Extra Innings

Extra Innings

The Joy and the Pains of Over-30 Baseball

by PATRICK SMITH

McFarland & Company, Inc., Publishers
Jefferson, North Carolina, and London

LIBRARY OF CONGRESS CATALOGUING-IN-PUBLICATION DATA

Smith, Patrick, 1966 Oct. 17–
    Extra innings : the joy and the pains of over-30 baseball /
by Patrick Smith.
    p.   cm.
    Includes index.

    ISBN-13: 978-0-7864-2909-7
    (softcover : 50# alkaline paper) ∞

    1. Baseball — United States — History.   2. Baseball players —
United States.   3. Middle-aged men — Recreation — United
States.   I. Title.
GV863.A1S674   2007
796.357 — dc22   2006102414

British Library cataloguing data are available

Cover photograph ©2007 Brand X Pictures

Manufactured in the United States of America

McFarland & Company, Inc., Publishers
Box 611, Jefferson, North Carolina 28640
www.mcfarlandpub.com

For Bob and Mal

Contents

Acknowledgments

Because they didn't know I was writing this book, I've changed the names of all the players, umpires and fans in the Over-30 League.

My teammates inspired me not only to tell this story, but to keep playing ball. The only bond that holds us together is baseball. But that's a pretty strong bond. I'm grateful to know and to have played with every one of them, particularly numbers 6, 7, 10, 16, 18, 22 and 69. They're the reason I come back each year.

Thank you to Kelly Smith, Donald Smith, Jeanne Smith, Curt Tilly, Luke and Eli, Jackson Mahoney, Wayne Laufert, Jean Paffenback, Matt McLaughlin, Lisa McLaughlin, Libby McLaughlin, John McComb, Alice Sowaal, Scott Perryman, Billy Brent Malkus, Matt Steigerwald and Chuck Tildon. Extra special, top-shelf thanks to Barbara Robinette Moss, Joe Krocheski and Lotta Olén.

Place an assist in the scorebook for the excellent BaseballReference.com and RetroSheet.com.

And, most of all, thanks to Deborah Shaller, whose patience, wisdom, wit and spirit have made my life bright for all these years.

One

===

Scott Abbott's back and he looks stoned. Not cold-medicine stoned, either. Stoned stoned. That's a fucking nerve. He dumped us last year for a team that was supposed to be good. Turned out, the Tigers were worse than the A's.

The A's. That's my team. And the only ones here are the six or eight guys who've got it the worst. We're the players who can't stay away on a freezing cold weeknight in the middle of winter, the ones who risk injury to take a couple swings off live pitching in a dark batting cage.

This isn't baseball, really. Baseball season is still months away. It's what passes for spring training in the Baltimore County Over-30 League. But "spring" is probably the wrong word. As is "training."

Freezing under buzzing florescent lights in a drafty warehouse in February, this isn't baseball weather. Smarter people are thinking about basketball and fireplaces. Nevertheless, here we are again. Baseball's back. Sort of.

In a far corner of the drafty metal barn, the old guy who runs the place watches a college basketball game on a black-and-white television. He leans almost too far back in his chair, his old-guy sneakers propped on a dented metal desk, a huge plug of tobacco straining against his cheek. Every few minutes, he aims a black stream of tobacco spit in the direction of a rusty Folgers coffee can in the middle of the cold cement floor. Sometimes the stream goes in the can, sometimes it doesn't, accounting for the steaming dark puddle that surrounds the can. Years ago, the caretaker was a right-handed pitcher for the Minnesota Twins. Tonight, he wears a Twins cap and rents faux pitcher's mounds and moldy batting nets by the hour to men too desperate to wait for warm weather.

1

Abbott sits the wrong way on a plastic chair, his faded green A's hat backward on his head, watching the television over the old-timer's shoulder. Eyes half-closed, Scott's transfixed, either by the game itself or by the bluish light glowing from the old TV with the crumpled aluminum-foil antenna. He rests an elbow on the chair's plastic back, head cocked, getting a better angle on the fingernail he's chomping. Neither man says a word until Sorenson shows up.

"Hey, good lookin'," Joe purrs to Abbott, slapping him hard on the side of the head. "You ready to get after it?" Abbott straightens his hat as his long body rises from the chair and meets Joe in an embrace.

"You know it, man," Abbott says, with a stoner's lilt. "Let's roll."

The old man spits at the can and never looks up from the TV. I sit against a far wall, with the rest of the A's, catching up on my teammates' lives since the last time we saw one another — a desperately hot day late last August. Tonight is so cold that summer seems impossible.

"OK, brdatdosls, et's git 'er goin'!" hollers DD, the A's manager. He's fifty-eight, works for the phone company and is largely unintelligible. I can understand maybe one of every four or five words DD says. I can only hope it's one of the important ones. I've seen three guys go to the mound at one time thinking DD sent them in to pitch. There have been days when the only words I understood from my manager were "if," "junk," "slider," and "fucker." DD is dragging an old, black canvas bag full of bats and catcher's gear across the warehouse floor.

Every winter, while the game hibernates, DD schedules workouts at this indoor baseball facility that has a wooden pitcher's mound and a saggy, stinky, shredded batting cage. It's a chance to swing a bat and loosen our creaky shoulders and elbows. But more important than that, it's a chance to think about baseball again, to be ballplayers. If we were honest with ourselves, we'd admit that the workouts don't really help our games much. But they remind us that baseball season is more than a dream. Some years, it gets so cold and the game feels so far away that you don't entirely trust your memories of last season. Did all that really happen?

The A's spring training isn't mandatory. In fact, with the A's, nothing's mandatory. A practice here, a practice there. Hey, whatever.

"Et's get 'er goin', 'en! C'mon!" DD's shouts echo off the cinder blocks and corrugated metal. The A's stir.

We pair off, one of each duo visiting the green plastic bucket full of last season's baseballs. The balls have distinct personalities and their color and texture tell their stories. The ones with smooth leather and worn down stitches got smacked around in hot weather games last year. The ruddy, scuffed-up balls that feel a little heavier than they should spent too much time in puddles. Each of the visitors to the ball bucket roots around for a ball that's just right.

After selecting a browned baseball, we instinctively fall into rows under the buzzing fluorescent bulbs, tossing the balls to our catch partners. Shoulders and elbows are startled to creaky life after months of slumber. Point your left shoulder and follow through with a step. Nice and easy. Each player groans with the first four or five throws. We windmill our throwing arms and jiggle our elbows, waking the tendons and muscles that have only just stopped hurting from last season. Soon, though, arms loosen and balls fly on straight lines, snapping loud into leather pockets.

The Lutherville (Maryland) Athletics are plumbers, demolition guys, investment bankers, security guards, salesmen. We'll all go to work tomorrow with sore arms. But the ache will remind us of baseball and it won't bother us.

When we're loose, a couple of us duck into a batting tunnel formed by a big cotton net hung from pipes in the ceiling. The black net sags a little in the middle, between the mound and the plate. I grab the first bat of the season and take some practice swings before I step into the fading batter's box painted on the concrete. A player new to the A's is on the fake mound, stretching his pitching arm across his body.

"You ready?" he asks.

I nod and take one last practice swing. The new guy starts into a gentle, natural windup. The first pitch of the season floats in, belt-high. I turn my hips and get all the way into it. I rip the pitch straight back up the middle, fizzing like an Alka Seltzer. The rookie leans a little and the ball whizzes past his head. "Nice shot," he smiles.

Despite the bad lighting, I'm seeing the ball clearly and hitting everything hard. I bought a new bat around Christmastime and it feels exactly right. A 33-inch metal Louisville Slugger, the bat has perfect balance and a huge hitting spot. I bat left-handed — one of two left-handed bats on the team. Besides the first shot back up the middle, I'm pulling the rookie's pitches toward what would be right field, if I wasn't hitting inside a trawler's net. At this point in the season, I never worry where I'm hitting the ball. I'm just glad to be hitting at all.

You can tell by watching the rookie's smooth pitching motion for a few minutes that he's a smart, talented ballplayer. He complains that he hasn't thrown a baseball in years, but he looks as natural as any of us. At least.

And I'm hitting everything he's laying up there. Despite an off-season of near total inactivity, I feel good, energetic.

You see the ball flying, almost floating in. You've started your swing from the bottoms of your feet. Turn your front foot a little and open your hips, like you're dancing. Your hands are last, pulling the bat through like a fishing net. Connect with the ball and feel that tiny resistance, that little push back. Feel it in your hands and nowhere else. If you hit it wrong, you feel it everywhere — wrists, neck, teeth, all over. But when it's right, the feeling's only in your hands.

The rookie's not trying to throw it past me. He's throwing perfect batting practice and I'm crushing every pitch he throws, one after another.

After about 20 swings, I step out of the batter's box and duck under the batting-cage net, breathing hard and sweating. I'm reminded of months of avoiding exercise.

The rookie also ducks under the net to let the next guy pitch. I introduce myself and we shake hands. He says "Hi. Rod Clement. Way to hit the ball."

"Hey, thanks." Wait. Did he just say his name is Clement? That's some serious baseball pedigree. I try to act cool, even though it's immediately obvious that I feel like I'm meeting a celebrity. Rod's dad was a legend.

Max Clement was a Baltimore Oriole during their greatest years. His team won the American League pennant in 1969 and 71 and the World Series in 1970. He shared the field with Brooks and Frank Robinson. Nobody would argue too much if you called that one of the best teams in the history of the game.

He also died not long ago. Only in his 60s, Max Clement had cancer that ravaged his body in no time at all. The whole city mourned when he died. When the rest of my team hears that the new guy's last name is Clement, the flood gates open. "Holy shit, dude!" "You mean, like, THE Clement?" "You any good?"

After Rod answers the millionth question from his new teammates about his dad and the old-time O's, he takes a quiet moment behind an old pitching screen to collect himself. To the rest of us, Max Clement was a legend we saw on TV and in the paper. To Rod, he was all that and a dad.

Abbott asks me if I wouldn't mind helping him get loose. I grab my catcher's mitt and a mask and squat behind a cracked home plate set up on a threadbare green mat that doesn't look anything like grass. While Abbott stretches his back and kicks at the pitching rubber, I settle behind the plate and try to remember why he left the A's last year. Oh yeah. Because his best friend moved in with his wife. And his best friend plays for the A's.

At first, when Joe and Julie started dating, the three of them were the only ones who weren't awkward about it. The rest of the A's were aghast. All last season, there were hushed conversations during warm-ups.

"Man, I'll tell you what. That is bad news," said Chris Nichols, grabbing a warm-up ball from a green bucket and flipping it to me.

"Abbott said he doesn't care," Alex Bell strained, laying in the grass and stretching his hamstrings. Alex was known to fool around a little himself. No one on the team had ever seen his wife, but more than a few different women came to A's games to watch the first baseman. "If he doesn't care, then what's the problem?"

"I don't care what he says, he cares," Phil LaSalle said, throwing a ball stiffly. "Scott and Julie have three kids. Even if Scotty doesn't care if Joe's balling his wife — and she's still his wife — you think it doesn't bother him that Joe comes home to those kids?"

I tossed a dirty baseball back and forth with Chris, thinking of Abbott's small boys, who act like tornadoes at the ballpark.

"Hey, if he says he doesn't care, what's Joe supposed to do?" Alex asked.

"I'll tell you what he's supposed to do," Chris yelled, pointing his mitt in Alex's direction. "Have the common damn decency to lay off his teammate's wife. That's what he's supposed to do!"

"Shhh! Jesus, dude! Keep it down!" LaSalle whispered urgently.

Abbott spent last year with the formerly good Tigers. Consensus around the league was that, with Abbott, the Tigers would be unstoppable. But they came completely unglued. The A's eliminated them in the second round of last year's playoffs, rocking Scott in the late innings. The game was tense and Scott threw a few balls a little too close to our chins. We kept our composure and hit Scott hard. After it was over, he interrupted our drunken post-game celebration and had to be dragged away from the taunting A's.

Now Scott's back with the A's and no one's explaining why.

In an instant, catching comes back to me. I forgot how much I like to catch Abbott. Sure, he dumped us last season for a team he thought would be better than the A's, but catching Scotty is like driving a Cadillac. He begins slowly, reintroducing himself to the mound, smoothing imaginary dirt with the bottom of his shoe. Steps a little with his left foot, turns his right foot against the pitching rubber, kicks his left knee while he ducks his head behind his left shoulder. Pushing off against the rubber, his momentum propels him toward me. Abbott uncoils as he throws. He's not throwing hard, but his pitches have a force behind them. He hits my mitt every time. I barely move.

Some people like to eat after they smoke pot. Others watch TV or listen to music. Abbott, evidently, likes to pitch.

Little by little, Scott revs the engine. My catcher's mitt lets go a loud "bang!" with every pitch. Effortlessly, he gets into a rhythm. Bang! Bang! My only job is to put up a good target and throw the ball back to him quickly and hard, so I don't disturb his groove.

Scott also lets you know what he's going to throw before every pitch. It's courtesy to let the catcher know what's coming. But you'd be surprised how many pitchers don't bother. Sliders and curveballs

6

carom off catchers expecting something straight, leaving bruises anywhere flesh is exposed. Not Scotty. He waves his glove across his body, indicating a curveball. He snaps off his first curveball of the season and it bends in a perfect arc. With full faith that the ball will come right to me, I'm perfectly still. Spinning like it's got a motor, the ball hits the pocket of my mitt. Bang!

Abbott throws for about 10 minutes and I feel that codependent connection catchers feel with pitchers. We need them. Sure, they need us, too, but it's different. Catchers are the homely girls who'll do anything to keep the prom king happy. Pitchers, especially good pitchers, always seem to be this close to breaking up with catchers.

When Scott's loose, we walk together back to the cage, slowly.

"Lookin' sharp," I tell him through my mask.

"Thanks," he says. He knows he looks sharp.

Then, through a stony haze, Scott Abbott acts like he just remembered something. "Oh yeah, dude—you ain't gonna be doin' much catchin' this year. We got somebody else."

Wait a minute. What? But I'm the catcher. I made the all-star team last year as a catcher. And what the hell is he talking about? He wasn't even here last year. What the fuck? Did he say "we" got somebody else? Since when is Abbott making decisions on this team? Why am I not hearing this from the manager?

"Who got somebody else? You? What are you talking about?" I sputter.

"Naw, forget it. DD'll tell you about it," he says walking away, without even bothering to say it in my direction.

What kind of bullshit is that? Abbott's news, delivered with such authority, made me furious. But I'm hung up between being a civilized adult with a wife and a job and a mortgage and being a declining—but desperate—ballplayer.

I hate being part of a plan and then not told about it right away. But I guess, everyone hates that. It's like being a child again, feeling left out of an important secret that involves you. In the rest of my relatively well-adjusted life, I wouldn't listen to bullshit like Scott's. I'd either call him on it or decide to leave the whole issue alone. It's not worth it.

But as a ballplayer, I don't do anything. I'm silent and wait to hear news about my own fate from my team's manager.

As far as I can tell, DD's managerial responsibilities are limited to two thankless duties: making phone calls reminding the A's to show up for the game and dragging a canvas sack full of baseball bats out of a metal shed. Joe is the leader of this team. He's spent the last two or three seasons denying it, sneaking around reversing his stepfather's managerial decisions. But the whole team knows it. If you've got some kind of problem, if you're not playing your favorite position, or you're not hitting high enough in the order, Joe is the guy to talk to. And he'll be the guy to tell you to go to hell.

A brute who refuses to acknowledge any authority outside of his own muscles, Joe Sorenson owns a company that will destroy anything you ask it to. The Crush Corporation is known around the region as the company to call when you want something flattened. Built like his demolition company's wrecking ball, Joe has an explosive temper.

Last season, he was arrested for drunk driving in Cooperstown, N.Y., and landed in jail for refusing to follow his arresting officer's orders. A visit to the Baseball Hall of Fame was followed by many, many beers and a series of bad decisions. When he got pulled over, Joe didn't bother to flee the scene. He just stood there, drunk and defiant, refusing to get into the squad car. The unfortunate officer was a woman and Joe simply would not be hauled to jail by a woman. In Baltimore or New York City, a cop would stun him or mace him or something and stuff his ass into the car. But in Cooperstown, she just kept asking politely.

The longer the episode lasted, the two of them standing by the side of the road in a standoff, the more amused Joe became. "I just figured I was already fucked," he said when he finally got back. "Might as well have some fun at it." To Joe, taunting a small-town police officer was fun. The policewoman tried to turn Joe around and handcuff him, but the wide man would not budge. She tried other maneuvers, like twisting an arm behind his back, but Joe just stood there, laughing. The harder she tried, the harder he laughed. That's what finally did it, Joe said. He laughed so hard as she climbed all over him that he became

8

incapacitated. She never did get handcuffs on him, but did manage to shove him into the car long enough to call for additional help. Joe spent a couple nights in the Cooperstown jail and had to go back for a hearing around Christmas.

I mope around for the rest of the spring-training workout, angry at Scott for assuming some kind of leadership position on the team after abandoning us; angry at DD for going along with it; and angry at myself for caring.

I try hard to forget Scott's pronouncement that I've lost my catcher's job. What the hell did he know? But part of me knows he's right. He didn't make it up. It had to come from somewhere.

Two

I've never hung around much with baseball players. I can only think of a couple teammates I was ever really friends with. Day after day, at home and at my job, I'm a friendly, outgoing guy. I have lots of friends. People tell me I'm funny.

But as a member of a baseball team, I'm sullen, sulky, and paranoid. I don't know what it is, but I've always been much moodier on the ball field than as an ordinary citizen. People say baseball's great because you can fail two-thirds of the time and still be an all-star. Yet, all that failing gets to a player after a while. It gets to me, anyway.

Baseball fools me every off-season. Each winter, I become convinced that I'm the type of player and fan who merely enjoys the game; appreciates its art and its beauty without getting too hung up on wins and losses, or hits and errors. But as soon as Opening Day rolls around, I remember: more often than not, baseball's painful.

Every day, on couches all across America, grown men tell mental health professionals about their fears of rejection. And those fears begin with Little League baseball tryouts. I imagine Ted Williams didn't worry much about Little League tryouts. But the rest of us did.

I don't remember much about my first tryout. Only the traumatic parts. I was eight and I bawled my head off the night before, asking my dad what would happen if I didn't make the team. "Don't worry about that," he said. "Just have fun." I guess he thought that would help. Fun? What was fun about this?

I guess I did OK the next day. I made the team and played an unremarkable year. Season after season went by and tryouts got easier, less traumatic. But now, returning to baseball after being away for so long, I felt like an eight-year-old again. I didn't cry the night before the over-30 tryout, but I did ask my wife what would happen if I didn't make the team. "Don't worry about that," she said. "Just have fun."

I guess she thought that would help.

In high school, when everything else was new and scary, a baseball dugout was exactly where I belonged. Not in the game right now? Sit back, pull your cap down low, cross your legs at the ankles, get yourself a little chew and enjoy the game. Spit wherever you like.

And, for better or worse, being a high school ballplayer entitled you to benefits available to few other students. Since football and basketball games were at night and on weekends, those players never missed class. Baseball games, however, started at 3:00 p.m. For most away games, that meant leaving class at noon to get dressed and get on the bus. The clack of metal cleats in the hallway meant you were on your way to the ball field. No one was authorized to stop you in those things.

I loved the pace of the game and the way it gently stimulated all five senses. I loved the way my hands felt after catching nine innings; dry and dirty and smooth, smelling like my soft, leather catcher's mitt. Baseball on a hot day made sweat run like a waterfall from every part of my body, soaking my uniform, cap, socks and shoes. A cleansing, a baptism, a stinky union with the dusty diamond. Baseball on a cold day meant a snappy turtleneck under my jersey, a cozy warm-up jacket and hot coffee in the dugout.

I played other sports. Some basketball and football. But I was pretty lousy at both, maybe because I hated the torturous practices. Basketball practice involved sprint after sprint, until someone emptied his stomach onto the court. Football practice was running in the Carolina heat inside a suit of armor.

Baseball practice was fun. It was ground balls and chatter and infield practice, followed by an hour-and-a-half of standing around in the sunny outfield, cap on backwards, sunglasses on, jogging in the grass after batting-practice fly balls and showing off for any girls who might be watching.

Once, in the eleventh grade, the wrestling coach asked me to try out for his team. As he spoke, I remembered seeing those tormented souls practice. On a beautiful sunny day, the wrestling coach would have these kids running as hard as they could, wearing some kind of rubber suits. They had burns on their faces from the sticky mats they rolled around on. Wrestlers were so concerned about pre-match weigh-ins that they'd take pills that made them pee too much. And rather than swallow their bodies' own natural water, they'd spit into plastic/foam cups, just to drop those last few ounces before the weigh-in. I always wondered, how much can spit weigh? I told the wrestling coach no thanks. I refused to participate in any sport where the weight of your saliva was an issue.

Like most ballplayers, I stopped playing when I went to college. Who had time for baseball when there was all that dope to smoke? From spring to summer to fall, each year since I was eight, I'd played baseball. By 18, I was ready to put the game away. And I didn't miss it much at the time; no more hot, infected strawberry-knee scrapes that took all season to heal. No more foul tips off the fingers. No more awful cups stuffed in your pants. I "studied" literature and became a lefty campus activist and had a radio show. Baseball seemed a long way off.

But as years passed and careers began and I no longer defined myself as a ballplayer or as an athlete, the game's mythology grew. Today, years later, despite an XXL waistline and bifocals, I've come back to the diamond.

A few years ago, I worked as a publicist for the American Red Cross in Baltimore, where I met a tiny man who was a champion blood donor. Every two months, this guy would roll up his sleeve and take that garden-hose needle in the arm. In its vaguely gruesome way, the Red Cross calculated all the blood this man had donated during his lifetime. His donations amounted to some outrageous quantity like 30 gallons of blood and I took aim at getting him a little credit in his neighborhood newspaper.

I interviewed the man and learned that, in addition to his ordinary job at some factory or other, he was commissioner of a baseball league for guys 30 and older. I'd thought about playing in some kind of hardball league, but I always found an excuse not to. Too intimidating. I hadn't played ball since high school. Can you imagine, I asked myself, what I'd look like stuffed into a baseball uniform today? Yikes. The commissioner blood donor assured me that, while the league was competitive, nobody was all that good. If I knew anything about playing the game, he said, I'd be fine. He himself, despite his superhuman ability to regenerate red blood cells, was no specimen. At most, the guy weighed 150 pounds. He was short and wore huge glasses. I figured him on the long end of his forties. I was 32 and kind of, uh, beefy. Working at various desks for the past 15 years had caused the contents of the package to shift and settle. But if this guy could do it, I was pretty confident I could too.

I was right.

And I was wrong. I learned how to hit and field again. I remembered how to run the bases and my throwing arm slowly returned. But I've never done what, once I was in the league for a year or two, I thought I'd be able to do. I'm just not as good as I was before I stopped playing. Happily, neither is anybody else.

The first day four years ago wasn't called a tryout. They called it an "evaluation." If you paid your $140, you were guaranteed to be assigned to one of the league's ten teams. Still, I was sick with nerves. Nobody wants to look like an oaf in front of a lot of strangers. And even if I was sure to be placed on a team, I was terrified that I'd completely suck and get picked last.

Well, I did suck. And I might've gotten picked last. Happily, I'll never know. There was some sort of secret-ballot draft among the league's managers. I don't suppose I was the worst that day, but I was pretty awful.

It was like being eight again. And not in a good way. Suddenly any personal or professional accomplishments I might have enjoyed since high school meant nothing. What mattered was how hard I could throw and how well I could hit. This tryout, this evaluation, this whatever-you-want-to-call-it, didn't allow me to put on a necktie and speak authoritatively. At various jobs, I've learned how to get professional respect from people who've never seen any work I've produced. I can wear a starchy shirt, call a meeting and use trendy business buzzwords.

14

On a baseball diamond, you have to prove it. No one is exempt. To gain any kind of credibility with managers and teammates, you've got to perform. Everyone's batting average starts at .000. As I was about to take the field for the first time in 15 years, I wished I'd realized all this a little sooner.

But I never do. Fantasies gallop out of control in the weeks and days before I get into something new. I never imagine myself nervous or sick to my stomach, though that's how it always turns out. I see myself succeeding. Not in the motivational-speaker "envisioning" kind of way. More in a daydreamy, stupid way. Whatever the new endeavor might be — maybe it's a new job, maybe it's some kind of presentation — my gauzy dream version of it always ends with me getting carried around on people's shoulders like Joe Paterno after the Sugar Bowl. I always see myself making that corny gesture with my hands clasped together, pumping on either side of my grinning mug. What's that called, anyway?

When the time comes to deliver the goods, though, daydreams abandon me. Great doubt moves in, and I question every decision I've made leading up to the new thing.

In the middle of a muddy ballfield, I had a new daydreamy fantasy: running away.

The field was thick with mud after a cold rain, but it looked great, like a kid's baseball-themed birthday cake. Fences all the way around, with bright yellow piping on the top around the outfield. There were foul poles and distance signs — 333 down the lines, 405 to dead center.

I'd gone out of my way to drive past the field a couple times the week before the evaluation. Mixed in with my wild fantasies of baseball heroics were a couple of anxiety dreams of driving around in a panic, late for the evaluation, unable to find the field while other new guys were impressing the managers and getting drafted. Though it wasn't more than three miles from my house, I made sure I knew the best route to get there and exactly how long it would take.

Evaluation day was a cold, steely gray Saturday, the middle of March. During the week, Baltimore had endured a few days of what weathermen call "the wintry mix," kind of half-rain, half-sleet. The night before the evaluation, a misting, foggy rain soaked the ground.

Baseball seemed remote. It was too early to be playing ball in this part of the country. The day was more likely to bring snow than any kind of baseball weather. The Orioles were still a couple weeks away from decamping their Florida baseball paradise. If major leaguers won't play in this kind of weather, wheezing guys with sore arms shouldn't either.

For weeks, I thought about what to wear that day. I was tempted to go nuts and buy some kind of expensive uniform and look really sharp at the evaluation. But that would be pretty dangerous. Nothing says "Greetings from Dorkville!" better than a no-hit, no-field ballplayer with a fancy uniform. Sensibly, I decided to go another route — the shabby hardball-chic route.

I went to one of those enormous sporting goods places and bought a pair of white, extra-large baseball pants, a black stretchy belt and an oversized Cincinnati Reds T-shirt that said "Griffey 30" on the back. Cool.

I mentioned the pants were extra-large. But extra-large what? Apparently, sporting goods manufacturers' definition of extra-large differed a little from, say, Lands End. Styles had changed since the 80s, the last decade I'd worn a uniform. Baseball pants weren't worn skintight anymore. There was supposed to be a little room in the pants. But my $12.99 polyesters hugged me tighter than my grandmother.

As a boy, I had a baseball card depicting a slender, effete-looking Houston Astros outfielder named Greg Gross. On the card, Gross was posing as though he'd just finished a half-hearted swing. Brightly colored by his yellow, red, orange and gold Astros jersey, Gross's torso was slightly twisted from his follow-through. In that odd pose, Gross looked like someone had dipped his lower extremities in white paint. His pants were tighter than Pat Benatar's. He must have needed a shoehorn and a can of Crisco to get them on.

My new baseball pants weren't that tight. But Greg Gross and Pat Benatar were never far from my thoughts all day.

A player's hat says everything at a baseball tryout. My new Ken Griffey shirt tempted me to go all the way and get a Reds hat. Just like that, instant Cincy look. But imagine what a complete putz I'd look like, dressed exactly like Ken Griffey at an over-30 evaluation. The whole get-up would've looked too careful. Sent the wrong message.

So, plan B: the Orioles hat. I'm an Orioles fan. I have three or four Orioles hats — new ones, old ones, classic cartoon bird, ornithologically correct bird. Take your pick.

But alas, the unwritten rule of baseball fashion prohibits doubling up on big league gear. You may not wear the stuff of two different major league teams at one time, even if their colors happen to match (which, in this case, they didn't). The Reds shirt meant no O's hat. And anyway, everybody in the league lives in Baltimore. We're all Orioles fans. We're all liable to wear Oriole hats to the evaluation. That would just look silly.

So how about the University of Maryland Terrapins? Nope. Too high.

By too high, I mean it sat too high on my head, like a politician who wears a hat that somebody hands him during a campaign. "Look! He's a Maryland fan! Whoo, Terps! I'm votin' for that guy!" Those hats just look dumb, like you're trying to pull something off and it's not quite working.

My last chance was a raggy, sweat-stained, bright red North Carolina State Wolfpack hat that sat real low on my head. Like the little cap Beaver Cleaver wore in about 1957. This low style of hat, thankfully, is back in fashion. Nearly every time I see one, I buy it in case they stop making them tomorrow. This NC State hat is broken in perfectly. And since the "double-up rule" doesn't apply to cross-cultural gear, a big league baseball/college basketball look was fine. I was in business.

I suited up for the evaluation and realized I hadn't purchased baseball shoes. I'd completely forgotten. So the whole purposeful look — the Griffey shirt, the cool hat, the new pants — was in peril until I found a pair of black sneakers in my closet. The shoes weren't made for baseball, but they sort of looked like they might have been. Crisis averted.

On evaluation day, the grass on the field was slick and shiny. The infield dirt wasn't dirt at all. It was thick, red mud. I was immediately glad I hadn't worn baseball shoes because after the first step on that field, players' cleats were full of soggy earth. The bottoms of my shoes were smooth and didn't hold mud as firmly as cleats.

There were ten or twelve new players to be evaluated and drafted that day. Warming up was tough, not just because of the weather, but because I hadn't warmed up for anything since I was 18. I mean, pickup basketball and some Frisbee, but nothing that required exercise to loosen a particular muscle. How was it done? I flailed my arms around a little, rolling my head around like I'd seen major leaguers do before games. I remembered seeing them jog or sprint in the outfield, so I found a spot down one of the foul lines to jog. I could feel the gallery of managers already watching from the metal bleachers behind the first-base bench, trying to see if any of the new talent knew what it was doing. I didn't, but I felt pretty confident that I looked like I did.

Running in the squishy, waterlogged outfield soaked my shoes and socks within seconds. Before I even picked up a glove, my shoes were done for the day. And it was raining. As an adult, I'd avoided doing anything in the rain, especially a cold rain. My body was conditioned to find cold rain repulsive. My Ken Griffey T-shirt was getting heavier each minute the misty rain continued. Gross.

I played catch with a big-bellied guy who had a catcher's mitt. I had trouble getting my arm loose and made my warm-up partner leap for the ball a few times. He'd time his jump just right, swing his arms once for leverage and heave himself about four inches off the ground. His jumps looked higher because he'd kind of kick his legs forward, jackknifing to give himself an extra boost as he reached his left hand as high as he could. He'd pick the ball out of the air and land heavily on his feet in the wet grass. He was polite about my wild throws, as I apologized and jiggled my arm around, trying to loosen it after 15 years. My partner wasn't any better. His throws had some zip on them, but they were all over the place. I chased as many balls as I caught. The wet baseball got heavier and heavier.

Finally, a guy who identified himself as having something to do with the league called all the players together near the pitcher's mound. From 80 or 90 feet away, my warm-up partner gave me the universal sign that he was as loose as he was going to get, sort of a miniature version of an umpire's safe sign. "I'm good," he said.

While I sloshed across the muddy field, I wondered, "Am I loose? Is this what loose feels like? I can't remember."

The guy from the league told a circle of new guys gathered around him how the evaluation would work. Basically, it was batting practice. One guys hits, another guy's on-deck, everybody else in the field. They'd look at our hitting and our fielding. Pitchers and catchers would work out on a little bullpen mound and home plate that were set up over by the batting cage down the right field line. Then, they'd bring the catchers onto the field to see how well they could throw.

Warm-ups had me feeling a little more confident, if only comparatively. My throwing partner certainly wasn't an all-star. And up close, the other guys at the evaluation weren't all that intimidating. So I thought I was prepared when it was time to let the league's managers take a look at me.

But I wasn't. When it came time to actually be "evaluated," I froze. Suddenly lonely and self-conscious, I fought hard to resist the impulse to get in the car and drive home. The weather was miserable. I'd go home and tell my wife I changed my mind; that the whole thing was a stupid idea anyway.

I'd done that before; left before a tryout was over. I was 21 and the Baltimore Orioles held a Saturday morning open tryout at my college. I had no money, a dry-rotted glove, a hangover and about 40 extra pounds. The guys who conducted the tryout wore actual Oriole uniforms with their last names on the back. They carried clipboards and kept looking at stopwatches. And the hundreds of players attending the tryout were younger and better-conditioned than me. The guys with clipboards and stopwatches divided players into positions and told us to line up on the right field foul line and face toward center field. One of the guys in an Oriole uniform blew a whistle and the whole crowd of players shot off the line in a sprint. It was only then that I realized what we were doing. It was a 40-yard dash and we were being timed. The slowest guy was 10 yards off the foul line by the time I figured out we what we were doing. Why was I the only one who didn't know what was going on? Paralyzing anxiety, that's why. I was too busy scolding myself for being there at all. After all, did I really think I had a chance to sign a contract? To get paid to play ball? I was still half-drunk from the night before. Who on earth told me I was... Wwhheeeeee! The whistle blew and off they went. I woke up, did my sprint and finished last. And then, as batting practice started, I picked up my stuff and walked home.

That was the last time I put on a uniform.

Until this day. When they asked, I told the managers who were running the evaluation that I was a catcher and a third baseman. And that was true. Fifteen years ago.

One of them told me that, since teams in this league never had enough catchers, they'd put me behind the plate for the evaluation. In the years since I'd strapped on all that gear, I'd forgotten two things.

First, I forgot that catchers have to wear larger-sized pants if they want to do all that crouching without the tops of their asses making an appearance.

The second thing I forgot is just how far it is from home plate to second base and how strong a catcher's arm has to be to make that throw. I never had a great arm, even when I was younger. But during the evaluation, after four or five feeble heaves to second, I felt like someone set fire to my right elbow. Each anemic throw took every shred of muscle I had.

My pants riding lower and lower, I asked myself why I was doing this?

Because I don't like softball.

I watched my dad play softball when I was a kid and the game seemed like an acknowledgement and acceptance of mortality. Forty-five feet from home plate, from a flat surface, a pitcher lobs a dead ball as large as a grapefruit toward the plate on a ridiculous arc. The catcher doesn't even need equipment. The batter waits, waits, waits, and swings with all his might. Klunk. Fly ball? Let's hope one of four outfielders can run it down.

Softball has none of baseball's crispness. Batters' hands never sting. The ball never snaps into a glove the way a baseball does. And the ball itself—wound so loosely that it won't bounce off cement. Instead of a bat's loud crack—or even the sharp "ping" of aluminum—a hitter who connects with a softball hears only a thump. Like beating dust out of an old rug on a clothesline.

When full-size adults put on uniforms and take to tiny softball diamonds, the proportion looks all wrong, like a Japanese monster

20

movie where Godzilla crushes tiny scale models of Tokyo. The uniforms themselves are another story. Snug, inorganic, stretchy short pants. Shirts tucked tight into underwear, a second skin over rounded bellies. Socks pulled high. White shoes.

Baseball players don't play a modified version of the game. They play the game itself. They take leads on the bases, they pitch from the stretch, they foul off as many pitches as they want, they throw as hard as they can.

Over-30 hardball is for guys who've never stopped playing, as well as guys who haven't played in years. It's real baseball on a regulation diamond — 90-foot bases and huge outfield expanses. Most players new to the league haven't touched a baseball since high school. This is my fourth year in the league. I've gotten a lot better since picking the game back up. But that's like saying you're thrilled with the progress you're making on that whole Nobel Prize thing.

I hit a few balls hard at the evaluation, but they noticed my catcher's mitt more than they noticed my bat. At one point, one of the managers asked me to do a "soft toss drill." Uh... sure. Turns out, the soft toss drill is when a batter hits balls into a small net a few feet in front of him. A guy sits just off to the side and tosses balls softly toward the batter. Get it? Soft toss is tossing softly. It's simple, really. Only the balls come at the batter from an angle he's not used to. Or, at least I wasn't used to it. It's like standing at home plate and having the pitcher throw from the dugout. A ball coming from the side, toward the hitter's midsection — no matter how softly it's tossed — is virtually impossible to hit. Let me rephrase: I sure didn't hit any that day. Not one. I swung and missed at least 30 times, failing to put bat to ball even once. Oddly, the soft-tossing manager didn't draft me.

Once I got to the actual plate, hitting off actual pitching, I didn't do much better. I guess all that soft toss made a mess of what little hitting technique that remained after a decade-and-a-half of no baseball. I hit one or two balls hard, but mainly I hit grounder after grounder to the right side of the infield, rolling my left wrist over. What could the managers possibly think of a short, slow guy who hit one ground ball after another? Any team that needed a likely double-play candidate couldn't go wrong drafting me.

21

But my defense wasn't half bad. And for that, the credit goes to my catcher's knees.

Lord knows, I have more than my share of afflictions. I've always fought weight problems. Well, maybe I haven't fought them, exactly. I have flat feet. I'm prone to get a sore shoulder after the first few weeks of the season. I'm even bald. But one thing — or two things, really — that I'm fortunate to have are healthy knees.

I can squat down and catch forever. I'm pleased to report I have no knee problems — a rarity in the Over-30 League.

Catching doesn't bother my knees at all. It can be tough on my hips and, early in the season, it hurts the bottoms of my feet. But the knees are fine. So, at the evaluation, I strapped on the catcher's equipment and warmed up pitcher after pitcher. I even caught most of batting practice. I figured at least managers would see I was durable, even if I couldn't hit.

After the evaluation was over, I made sure to help put away the bats and muddy baseballs. Everybody likes a "team guy." We were supposed to go home and wait to hear which team had drafted us. My chunky warm-up mate wished me luck. "Thanks," I said. "You too."

The rain picked up as I walked to my car, stiff from using muscles that had been dormant since the last time I played baseball. At my car, I took my soaked shoes off and clapped off the mud, which splattered all over the side of my car. The wet shoes sounded like boulders when I threw them in the back. Sitting in — and dripping all over — the driver's seat, I felt like a ballplayer for the first time in years. I steamed up the windows and smiled.

I drove home to wait for a phone call. "Well?" Deborah asked. "How was it?"

I told her about soft toss and about catching and about warming up and about my sore arm. I think she could tell I'd had a good time.

A few hours later, the phone rang. "Is this Smith? Welcome to the A's," the voice said. "I'm DD and I drafted you today."

"Wow! That's great! Thanks... what'd you say your name was?"

"It's Dan. But everybody calls me DD. Anyway, welcome to the A's. We got a pretty good bunch of guys." He paused. "Y'know, sometimes they're a little high-strung, but they got good hearts. Mostly."

I didn't say anything. If I let him keep going, he might renounce his team altogether.

"Nah, nah," he corrected his faint praise. "They're OK. We might not win every game, but we'll have fun playing ball. Usually."

I thanked DD and he told me we'd play some kind of practice game the next day. I told him I'd be there.

When I hung up, I was imagining myself in an A's uniform when my wife came into the room.

"Who was that?"

"Honey, guess what! I'm an A!"

She didn't blink. "I've always known that."

Three

═══════════════════════════════

When Deborah's mother was dying in a hospice and we had only
to wait through her last days, Deb and I sat on either side of her bed
and watched the Orioles sweep an early season weekend series against
Kansas City.

The team looked good. The last win of the four-game set actually launched Baltimore over the .500 mark. They hit for power, they
delivered in the clutch, the starting pitchers went deep into games.

Deb's mother was awake during those late-spring days. I brought
breakfast from a bagel shop and she drank orange juice from one of
those bendy straws. We left the doors of her room open and a soft
breeze blew in and carried away the morphine-heavy hospice air. Deb's
dad stayed all day, showing up at dawn to guard his wife from death.
By the evenings, though, each parent was exhausted from the tangle of
never quite saying goodbye to one another, never acknowledging the
end, shuffling all around the inevitable.

He'd wait until Deb and I came back after work, then he'd go
home. I put the game on. While the Orioles took care of business
against Kansas City, the three of us chatted about how nice everyone
was at the hospice.

She'd fall into a light sleep in the early innings. Each night, Deb
and I watched the game while her mom dozed off, talking to each other
across the deathbed, sharing workday anecdotes. We made grocery lists
and talked about things like oil changes, as if we thought banality
would keep her mom alive.

Then the Orioles lost two of three in Tampa Bay. Deb's mom's
condition declined. She slept almost all the time. She no longer wanted
to drink juice from the bendy straws. The games in Tampa Bay were

25

as quiet as the hospice room. On television, the dome in St. Petersburg looked dark and empty. The Orioles were out of sorts. And when their closer gave up a three-run walk-off homer in the second game of the series, it felt like a little piece of life disappeared over the fence with the home run ball.

The Orioles lost again the next night in Tampa Bay, but with much less drama. After a three-run first inning, the O's couldn't muster another run all night. They lost 6–3.

The hospice people worked hard to keep Deb's mom comfortable. A combination of illness and medicine made her unconscious. We talked to her, told her we loved her, told her it was OK to go.

Finally, Baltimore got swept in Cleveland and my wife's mother died.

Don't misunderstand me. I don't tie the outcomes of a handful of ballgames to the end of a beautiful life and the devastating loss of a parent. I understand that Deb's mom wouldn't have lived any longer had the Orioles found a hot streak. But for me, the rhythms of the games never felt closer to the rhythms of life.

The results of those Oriole games against the Royals, the Devil Rays and the Indians weren't important. What was important was that the games were played. The Orioles were the only thing that made sense. Win or lose, those ordinary games had a narcotic cadence. Each night during the most difficult of times, the games rocked us to sleep. They provided a structure to evenings that otherwise would've been spent staring terrified at a dying mother.

Baseball teaches us to heal and to look to the future. When you're down today, tomorrow will be brighter. By the time the funeral came around, the Orioles were on the west coast, where they split six games with Oakland and Seattle.

I like football and basketball. But I don't mark the passage of time by football and basketball games.

Football games are only once a week. The games are entertaining and, heaven knows, I watch them. But I can't know the stories I'm interested in when I watch football. I know what the ball carrier did. But I don't know who did what to help him. Two gigantic linemen square off, each with the idea of imposing his will on the other. After the ball is snapped, one of those linemen wins and one loses. Football's full of epic battles. But we almost never know about them.

Basketball is better. I can see what's happening on the court. But, like football, the game is so bound by the clock that its stories get overwhelmed.

I love the way every baseball game is part of a series. When your favorite team's on the road, they'll play three or four games in a row against the same team. There's a great stability in that.

Like one of those Russian dolls that has a bunch of smaller Russian dolls that fit inside it, baseball's dramas and narratives are layered one atop another. Within each season, there are series that are stories to be told. Within each series, each game has a conflict and a resolution. Within each game, every at-bat is a contest of wills. And within at-bats, each pitch is a unique story.

All these stories fit into neat compartments. Wins and losses, balls and strikes, hits and outs. Which isn't to say the game lacks nuance. Baseball's full of costly wins and productive outs. Sometimes the game stories are simple, sometimes they're complex.

Baseball has a hypnotic pulse. Each game has it and each season has it. It's like falling asleep on a train.

The game is virtually the same today as it was a century ago. Yes, there's the designated hitter and the ball's wound as tight as a Superball. But, from season to season, there aren't fundamental changes in the game, the way there are in basketball and football — and don't even start with me on hockey.

In the early 1980s, the NCAA decided there should be a three-point shot on a basketball court. As it turns out, it was probably a good idea, but it was a fundamental change in the way the game was played and strategized. Same goes for the shot clock. Basketball seemed to need one, since teams could get an eight or 10-point lead and the fans would begin filing out. Most people would agree that a shot clock has been good for basketball. But again, it's a fundamental change.

Football seems to have changes every year. In the NFL, coaches couldn't opt for a two-point conversion until 1994. Then, suddenly, there it was. Nobody remembers the last time baseball made a change to something as central as the way points are scored.

27

It's democratic. A Wednesday night game against Detroit means the same as a Saturday game in Yankee Stadium. And when the season's over, when the last out of the World Series is made, you can reflect on the long season. You can find themes and make some sense of things.

Playing the game stimulates your senses in a way that being a fan does not.

On the field, the game tastes like hot Gatorade, swigged from the bottle that's been rolling around in my car all week. It tastes sweet and dry, like the infield dirt. After a backhand flop for a ground ball, I get a mouthful of dirt. I spit it out, but it clings to my tongue and mouth, a sticky coating that's impossible to hawk up and out. The dirt crunches like glass between my teeth. The game tastes salty like the leather strings on my glove. When no one's looking, I chew on them. I've been doing that since I was old enough to wear a glove. Something makes those leather strings taste good.

It feels slick like Asp-R-Creme, which has a baby powder kind of smell. Asp-R-Creme on a sore arm is like slopping Crisco all over your shoulder and putting a shirt over it right away. The shirt sticks to the gooey balm and clings to your shoulder all day. Players in the Over-30 League have permanent grease stains on the throwing arms of their undershirts. But medicine for sore arms is better now than it used to be. When I was in high school, we used a barely-legal concoction called Kramergesic to loosen sore and stiff arms. It was some kind of cold-hot glue. You'd reach into a big plastic jar and scoop out three or four fingers of translucent yellow grease that smelled like an atomic version of Vick's Vap-o-Rub. Then, you smeared a whole handful of this crap all over your sore shoulder. The stuff didn't dissolve into your skin, like lotion does. It just sat there, coating your skin. Put your shirt back on. Then, look out. Your eyes well up from the fumes and your shoulder feels like it's frozen. Moments later, your whole arm is on fire and no one will sit next to you in the dugout.

Baseball sounds like metal cleats on concrete and asphalt. It sounds like the flag flapping in the wind. It sounds like "ping" of an aluminum bat. It sounds like Ice Cream Joe's beat up van, with the crazy clown painted on it, blaring "Pop Goes the Weasel."

Baseball has a smell. It smells like mold, more than anything else.

Mold in the batting cage net. Mold in the shed where the bases and chalk and wooden bats are kept. It smells like my giant baseball bag, full of sweaty catcher's equipment that I zipped up and tossed in my car. All week long, the sun beat on that car, cooking the rancid catcher's gear. The catcher's gear hisses as I unzip the bag. And stink isn't really the word. It's kind of pleasant, actually.

Baseball smells like my shoes. When we play the early game, the grass is still wet with dew. Soon, my shoes are soaked clear through. After the game, I have to throw my shoes in the car last, open a window a quick to keep the stinky feet smell from imprinting on my car's interior. If I don't get it in time, the smell will never go away.

Baseball smells like the portacrapper cooking in the sun behind the bleachers.

Baseball smells like rain and mud.

The game smells like hot, damp, fermenting cut grass. Sharp and sour. It smells like the exhaust from the tractor they use to mow the infield and outfield grass, then drag the infield with the scary spiked-metal thing.

It smells like the hamburgers the Browns grill after their games.

Baseball smells like my game hat. I buy a new hat before every season and wear it all year. By July, it's completely ruined with sweat and dirt. No longer a handsome hunter green, my hat fades to a kind of alien green and has weird, uneven white rings all around it—salt stains from the quarts of perspiration I produce during the course of an afternoon game. I have a theory that you can tell the temperature of yesterday's game by counting the rings on my hat.

When I think of the first years I played baseball, I feel impossibly old.

I don't consider myself a particularly old guy. That's why it seems to unlikely to me that I played on a team that wore flannel uniforms. I think I had to be among the last players to wear one, but the first baseball uniform I ever wore, when I was nine, was made of fuzzy brushed cotton. I played for the Telephone Pioneers, a team evidently sponsored by a group of benevolent and civic-minded telecommunications workers. Who knew?

29

When the coach of the Telephone Pioneers called me to tell me I'd be on his team, I thought it was a prank.

"Congratulations. You're a member of the Telephone Pioneers," a man with a husky southern accent greeted.

"Uh... sure, mister." I thought it was a version of "is your refrigerator running?"

"Let's see... Is this Patrick Smith?"

OK. This has gone far enough. I wasn't about to fall for this lame gag call. Time to turn the tables. "Maybe. Is this Pope Paul the Sixth?"

"Mmm... no." He was a little taken aback. "This is Howard Turpin. I'm the coach of the Telephone Pioneers in the Kentwood Park Little League. Are you Patrick?"

It figured that the only time I ever had the nerve to get smart-assed with a crank caller, the caller wasn't a crank at all.

"Oh, uh... yes. Yes, I am. Sorry. Um... what did you say the team was called?"

"We're called the Telephone Pioneers."

"Great!" Time for a very long pause. "What's that mean?"

"What does what mean?"

"'Telephone Pioneer.' What's that?"

I don't remember what he told me. I was too busy thinking about how many times I'd have to explain what a Telephone Pioneer was. If anyone asked me if I played ball, they'd surely want to know my team's name. Then, instead of Joe's Exxon or Willie's Exterminators, I'd say I played for the Telephone Pioneers. Then I'd have to explain what a Telephone Pioneer is. Or was.

Every spring for years and years, somebody who had something to do with the Raleigh Rec and Parks Department dragged a big box of Little League baseball uniforms out of a musty storage room and threw it in the trunk of some guy's car. In this case, the trunk belonged to Howard Turpin.

So after a couple of practices, Turpin gathered his team in the Kentwood Park parking lot, kids forming a semicircle around the back of his aging metallic chocolate brown Buick. The coach unlocked his trunk and it bounced open with a popping noise. The kids took a step

closer, getting a sniff of Turpin's car, which, like Turpin himself, s
like Burger King and Winstons. The coach wore a BanLon shirt
too small for his big gut, which hung over his belt. He leaned
first into his car's abyss of a trunk, the crack of his big white as
ing prominently out of his pants. Naturally, the Telephone P
pointed and laughed with a gusto unique to kids and butt jok
the laughing stopped when Turpin straightened up, hugging a b
board box in his arms. The box's heavy load strained against
tom, the flaps nearly unfolding. The lid was ripped open and
man tossed the box down onto the asphalt in the middle of th
circle. It landed with a dull thud. Turpin pulled up his pants a
over the box, digging through flannel. "Tony, see if this fits."
tossed a wisp of a shirt to Tony Hedgespeth, or "Sped" as t
called him. The shirt hit Sped in the face and wrapped arc
head. "Gross! This stinks!"

"Kristie, try this on," Turpin mumbled, flinging a shirt
the girls on the Telephone Pioneers.

Kristie wrinkled her nose. "Mr. Turpin, do you have ano
This one really smells."

Now Turpin was throwing shirts one after another at ea
Pioneers. A couple of kids looked like they might cry.

The uniforms had to be twenty-five years old. When I
uniform that Turpin threw, I held it up and inspected it like
kids were doing. It smelled like mothballs and was threadb
knees and ass.

"You got a good one," Turpin told me, with a wink. "N
Like Johnny Bench."

"OK."

It did smell pretty bad, but I liked it immediately, in
way I've always liked things that seemed a little out of date
it needed me. I had a feeling about this uniform that you
you see a dirty stuffed animal by the side of the road. Who I
it got there? Maybe it fell out of a car. The point is, it's i
anyone. But one-eyed and stuffing fall out of it, the toy h
heart. You know it's an inanimate object. You're not a fool
an object manufactured so that someone would love it. An

ignored, filthy, discarded — the opposite of love. You want — you need — to pick it up and take it home. Sew it up and wash it. Put it in your dryer with one of those things that makes it smell good. Save it.

My Pioneers uniform was sort of like that. My mom disinfected it, then she washed it three or four times until it looked like a set of winter pajamas. And while the uniform no longer stunk, it did carry an essence of sweat and dirt and rain and mustard and anything else it was ever exposed to. Flannel is like that.

As the season wore on, the uniform collected new smells and the frayed patches barely held on. The button-up jersey was worn smooth on the outside and full of thousands of tiny, unremovable fuzzies on the inside. The sleeves were too long; they were baggy and fell past my elbows. The uniforms drooped on our nine-year-old Pioneer bodies as if they were hung on scarecrows. The red pinstripes were long faded and bled into the in-between.

And no wonder. Sweat has nowhere to go inside flannel in the summer sun, so it soaks the fabric and rolls down into your socks and shoes. The uniforms were hot and itchy, like wearing full-body oven mitts.

Say what you want about them, though; those uniforms were durable. They held together, slide after slide, against all laws of physics and textiles.

They used to be white, I guess. Years of grinding red Carolina dirt into the shirts and pants had permanently stained the uniforms a soft orange. No one had even bothered to buy new stirrups socks for these poor old get-ups. Dry rot had robbed the red stirrups of any elastic snap. By the second inning everyone's socks fell down and the stirrups hung so loose that it was easy to trip over them.

The Telephone Pioneers' hats looked like relics — fuzzy red cotton with a white felt "TP" interlocked above the bill. A leather band wrapped around in the inside of the hats. But, naturally, the leather was dried out and crumbled from years of sweaty foreheads. When the Pioneer kids took off our hats, we had a single stripe of black crumbs above our eyebrows. Unlike other teams in that league, the Telephone Pioneers hats didn't have plastic backs. Everyone else wore adjustable hats with plastic snaps on the back. Not us. Today, they call them

fitted. Then, it was just queer. Our hats went, as one kid on the team complained, "all the way around."

When we took the field against the other teams in the league, the games looked incongruous. We looked like a depression-era team that dropped out of the sky into the 1970s, like a video game where you could pit the Big Red Machine against the Gashouse Gang Cardinals. Today, at least the Pioneers would have a cool retro look. Those jerseys would go for about 400 bucks now. But in those days, there were no throwback jerseys. They were just old as hell. Other Little Leaguers in 1975 wore double-knit polyester uniforms with puffed-out, mesh-backed hats. We had smelly, faded, beat-up uniforms that made us look like the Little Rascals. File them under "once-proud."

But the uniforms hadn't always been thrift-store outcasts. Years before, when the pants still had some elastic in them, some philanthropist who worked for the phone company sponsored a ball team and outfitted them with the handsomest of uniforms.

The uniforms seemed sad to me, like they were all that remained of someone's dream. I imagined a smiling phone-company middle manager with a skinny tie and Buddy Holly glasses who sprung for a whole set of snappy uniforms. With great civic pride, he had them emblazoned with the name of the organization he held so dear — the Telephone Pioneers. Maybe they all got their pictures in the paper. Then, years later, after the man in the Buddy Holly glasses was long gone, the raggedy set of 16 or 17 little baseball uniforms remained. We were his legacy.

What else did the Telephone Pioneers sponsor? And did it last as long as the baseball uniforms they bought? I never saw their name anywhere else around Raleigh. Just our uniforms. That always suggested to me that, whoever was behind the uniforms loved only baseball. And telephones.

The Kentwood Park Little League had only four teams and was always in danger of going belly up. Everything about the league was bad. Bad coaches, bad umpires, bad parents and bad politics. Desegregation had long been the law, but in North Carolina, a lot of people just ignored it. It was true at my elementary school and it was true in my Little League. Thus, Kentwood had three all-white teams and one all-black team. The white teams were named after sponsors — Telephone Pioneers, Ridgeway Opticians, the Rotary Club. But the black team was named after a neighborhood. They were just called "Method." The kids came from Raleigh's Method Road neighborhood and rode to the game together, hanging out the back of an ancient green pickup truck. They hung on as the truck rattled into the parking lot, stacked on top of each other, wrestling and yelling.

Method brought a robust cheering section to every game. It looked like the whole neighborhood came to a baseball game for nine-year-olds. And the Method crowd was into the game, too. An old man with big eyes regularly sat in an aluminum lawn chair behind the backstop, just a few feet from the teenage umpire. The guy heckled everybody, nonstop. He heckled the umpire, the opposing team and their parents. And he egged on the Method cheering section. Every call — and I mean every call — that didn't go Method's way brought a chorus of hoots and jeers down on the umpire, who was probably making about five bucks a game. One game between the Pioneers and Method, the umpire just left. He got sick of the big-eyed guy in the chair behind the plate and he left. He told the coaches, "you got a lousy league with four lousy teams. Lots of luck finding another umpire to take this kind of crap." And with that, he walked off.

A Pioneer parent volunteered to umpire the rest of the game. And the Method crowd heckled him even worse.

When our team won or lost a couple games by forfeit — I can't remember which — my dad promised that next year, we'd find a better league.

After some phone calls and asking around, we found a much better league. The West Raleigh Little League was loaded. It had two different skill levels and 10 teams in each one. The field had bright lights for night games and a fence with sponsor advertisements all over it. Everything about the West Raleigh league was spiffy.

And to be honest, I was glad to be rid of the burden of the Telephone Pioneers. It felt smothering. And not just because the uniforms were hot. The Pioneers and the Kentwood League were always the verge of shutting down. Everyone in that league seemed relieved when the season ended.

My new team in the West Raleigh League had a sponsor that actually sold consumer products: Kirby Vacuum Cleaners. Our team motto: "We really suck!"

In fact, all the teams in the West Raleigh League had sponsors I'd heard of. I always wondered if anyone else noticed that every team in the league seemed to have a companion team, a team sponsored by a company that seemed like a natural fit for another team's sponsor. For instance, Kirby Vacuums' companion team was Carolina Carpet. Makes sense, doesn't it? What are the odds that one league would have a team sponsored by a vacuum cleaner manufacturer and a team sponsored by carpet company?

But wait. It gets better. Dunkin' Donuts had a team. Pink and brown uniforms, just like the people who work at the doughnut shop. Their companion? Pine State Dairies. Doughnuts and milk. Not as perfect as carpet and vacuum cleaners. But still, very good.

Coca-Cola had a team. Pepsi Cola had a team. Naturally, they were fierce rivals.

Believe it or not, United Airlines had a team in the West Raleigh Little League. I always thought they were more exotic than Kirby Vacuums. And United's companion team? It was a minor stretch, but I always connected United Airlines to the Raleigh Firefighters.

West Raleigh was a much more suburban league than Kentwood. Except for Method's huge cheering section, very few parents came to Kentwood games. Those who did sat almost silent on the metal bleachers behind the backstop. The league had no electricity. It had a broken down feeling, like no one was really having much fun. It was no accident that West Raleigh's league was run by the Raleigh Exchange Club, a civic organization that seemed flush with money. Kentwood was run by the city of Raleigh and was neglected and under-funded.

The field at West Raleigh sat at the bottom of a big bowl, the infield half of which was rimmed with cement stairs with wooden benches nailed to them. There was a little picnic area down the right field line. It was all very idyllic. Parents brought little plastic baggies full of celery and carrots and oranges for kids. A cinder block concession stand sat at the top of the bleachers, crawling with players' younger brothers and sisters, stuffing themselves with candy and cokes.

Kirby's coach was Gary Taylor, a rail thin man with the thickest glasses I'd ever seen. His pointy adams apple stuck out as far as the bill of his green Kirby hat. But a dignified aura hung around Coach Taylor, which is what he insisted we call him. Next to the slouchy, smoking Howard Turpin, Coach Taylor looked like Bear Bryant.

Just about every coach I've ever had in any sport gave a speech on the first day of practice. And the speech is virtually the same. It's always a version of "I'm the boss here. Don't screw around and make trouble. If you do, you'll be sorry." Coach Taylor was the only guy I ever heard give the speech and mean every word of it. Except he wouldn't have said "screw around" to a bunch of kids. He'd say "fuss" or "monkey."

Before every game, Coach Taylor got the whole Kirby team down the left field line and had us all get on one knee. "Remove your hats," he'd say. "And let's recite the Lord's Prayer." And we did. Once, two of the Kirby kids couldn't stifle a giggle in the middle of the prayer. For no good reason, really. They just laughed. Taylor had them run three laps all the way around the field, right there before the game, in front of the kids' parents. And nobody said a word. That's when the whole team got the message not to mess with Coach Taylor's prayer.

He was soft-spoken, his gentle East Carolina accent curling around his words like kudzu. Coach Taylor had a quiet authority that told you he meant everything he said.

Coach Taylor must've had something to do with the National Guard, because Kirby practiced for hours upon hours in the blazing sun on the Armory Field across the street from the NC State campus. The gray dirt on the Armory Field felt as soft as powder. Ground balls left trails of smoke behind them, right into the fielder's gloves.

All summer long, Kirby took the dusty field every day, behind a big iron cannon that looked like it was holding Western Boulevard hostage.

We had a pair of Japanese brothers who were tremendous ballplayers. Hiroshi Shoji and his brother Takaki were outfielders and pitchers who were among the smallest kids in the league. Both were outfielders and their parents were professors at one of the local universities. Neither of the Shoji brothers spoke English, except for a few tame swear words and some snippets of the Lord's Prayer.

As a child, though I lived in the south, I worshipped at the altar of the Pittsburgh Pirates. I spent night after summer night in Raleigh furiously jiggling the AM dial to capture Pittsburgh's KDKA radio. At the top of every hour, while Milo Hamilton or Lanny Frattare "paused five seconds for station identification on the Pirates Radio Network," the station would play a hopelessly corny little jingle that stayed lodged in my head for whole seasons at a time. "Kay-Dee-Kay-Ay, Piiiiiiittss-burgh... the Bucs!" That's it. No verb. Just station, city, diminutive team nickname. If the conditions were just right, I'd get the game and it wouldn't fade. Most nights, though, the signal crackled in and out, inexplicably getting weaker and stronger and weaker again.

I admired the way the Pirates broadcasters understood the importance of silence, something that feels lost today. Milo and Lanny's broadcasts featured long pauses that meant, factoring in spring training and the postseason, this was one game out of a couple hundred. No need to get too excited. Of course, when I had trouble getting the radio signal, the pauses were maddening. I couldn't tell whether my radio's silence meant Milo and Lanny were being subtle or that KDKA had faded out.

"Now here's Stargell." Ten or 15 seconds of quiet. "He's two for three tonight with a homer and three RBIs." Their words brought the game into my bedroom, 500 miles away.

I loved the Pirates because my dad loved the Pirates. Everyone else I knew who cared anything about baseball was an Atlanta Braves fan. And I liked the Braves OK. But the Pirates were magical to me, like an extension of my father and his father. It felt like they were in my blood.

Until I was about 13, my dad and I made an annual pilgrimage to Pittsburgh for a weekend series against the Cardinals or the Expos or the Astros. He'd get the tickets in the winter, as soon as they went on sale and for months, I'd study the Cards' or Expos' or Astros' rosters, thinking about matchups against the Bucs.

When the city of Pittsburgh dynamited Three Rivers Stadium in 2003, most people who know anything about baseball — and certainly anyone who knows anything about architecture — cheered the blast. Pittsburgh, Cincinnati, St. Louis and Philadelphia built nearly identical multi-purpose downtown stadiums in the early 1970s, where big league baseball teams could share with those cities' NFL entries. It seemed like a terrific idea.

Who needs two giant sports venues when everybody can share one? And anyway, when Foghat or Bad Company or even Billy Graham comes to town, they'll have a place to do their thing too. It's almost quaint now.

Three Rivers and its brethren were cavernous concrete doughnuts, with five or six tiers of seating surrounding a pea-green carpet painted to look like a ballfield. When the time of year came for the Pirates to yield to the Steelers, somebody scrubbed the baseball lines off the carpet and painted a white football grid. And vice versa. Over and over and over again. Thus, even in the middle of May, when the Steelers hadn't stepped foot on the field for six months, the football grid lines at Three Rivers Stadium were almost as clear as the day they were painted on.

The field was like a placemat stretched over a concrete slab. Ground balls ripped through the infield and picked up speed on their way to the outfield. More than once, I saw balls that would've been double-play grounders on the grass and dirt of Los Angeles or Boston become RBI gappers in Pittsburgh.

On our trips to Three Rivers, my dad would consent to my hanging around the box-seat railing before the game, hoping one or two Pirates would visit.

My favorite moment with a big leaguer is the one I had when I was nine when I got a visit from one of my all-time favorite Pirates, Manny Sanguillen. Somehow, I was the only kid at the railing when Manny came over.

"Hello, Mr. Sanguillen!" Why I felt compelled to be so formal, I don't know. I was aware that his English wasn't perfect and I needed him to understand me. I think my enunciation might have been a little over the top.

"Hey hey!" he said back, looking for something I might be holding that he could autograph. I had nothing. "You got something for me to sign?" he asked in his thick Panamanian accent.

"Uh, no. I just wanted to shake hands," I told him, sticking out my hand.

Sanguillen smiled his big gap-toothed smile and took my hand. His huge hand was rough, his forearm as big around as most people's thighs. He had a catcher's mitt on the other hand, which he placed on top of my head. I disappeared under it. Sanguillen pulled me to the rail and gave me a big squeeze, his mitt still covering my head. His polyester Pirates jersey was scratchy against my face, smushed into the letters embroidered on his chest. "You a good keed," he said quietly. My Pirates hat got stuck in his catcher's mitt and he pulled it off my head when he let go of me. It tumbled over the railing and onto the field. Sanguillen bent over, picked it up and replaced it crooked over my hair. He gave me an extra tap on the side of my head. "You be good," he said, winking. He disappeared around a corner and into the Pirate dugout. I looked around. Did anybody just see that? Did that really happen?

I don't have the worst eyesight in the world, nor do I have the best. I wear eyeglasses pretty much all day. Reading, writing, driving, watching television.

But my glasses are very much not designed for anything athletic. They're bifocals and the frames are designed by some Italian fellow. Not for baseball.

So, on the ballfield, I do without my glasses. I've concluded that it's more dangerous to play wearing glasses than to play and not be able to see very well. I can still see what I'm doing. But really, it would be a good idea to get contacts or sports glasses or something.

In my first year in the league, I saw guy get hit in the glasses. Not good. Broken nose, little pieces of glass buried in his face.

You're thinking, why not just buy athletic glasses? Because if I do, I'm admitting that my eyes aren't going to get better.

I always preferred city league and rec league baseball to teams connected to schools. Most of the games were in the summer, which in junior high school seemed like a lifetime. I played on those teams only for fun. That sort of baseball was about as far from school as I could get.

After Little League, I played in a great Babe Ruth league in downtown Raleigh for a team sponsored by a pharmacy. The switch from a league where players were between nine and 12 to a league where players were 13 and 14 was enormous. Little League ball is full of kids who play because it's something kids do. They're not particularly attached. But kids who played in this league all wanted to be there.

Hayes Barton Pharmacy was an OK team. We had two coaches who knew plenty about the game, Alton Sparrow and Hinky Jessup. Both were genial southern gentlemen, but Sparrow absolutely tortured his own kid, our centerfielder. Alton Junior was miserable and looked like he hated his chubby dad. Jessup, on the other hand, had a son whose first name was Smith. Smith Jessup was a goofy, doughy first baseman who had curly yellow hair and ran stiff-legged, like the Frankenstein monster. Hinky looked old enough to be Smith's great grandfather and said he'd played triple-A ball in Denver in the '50s.

I was the third baseman for Hayes Barton Pharmacy and I had a decent enough year. My coaches liked my game well enough to leave me in there. Strangely, though, it was another team's coach who paid real attention to me that year.

Alan Householder was a foulmouthed dwarf. He had short arms, short bow legs and made swearing an art. He coached Golden Skillet in Raleigh's Oakwood League and they handled Hayes Barton Pharmacy every time they played us. I must've done something in those games, though, because Householder picked me for the league's all-star team. In city-run rec leagues, the regular season is over by June. All-star teams get picked at the end of the season and usually go on little barnstorming tours, playing in tournaments for the rest of the summer and into the fall.

The next season, Householder coached in a different league and brought me with him. My parents were eternally grateful to him for getting me into a league closer to home; I could walk to the ballpark, saving them a whole summer's worth of trips across town.

Alan was polite and charming around my parents. Which was great, because when they weren't around, he was the cussinest, spittinest midget in west Raleigh. My parents liked Alan, despite his long scraggly hair, his beard and his b.o. He wore torn jeans and dirty T-shirts. He looked like he should've been in a miniature Lynyrd Skynyrd.

He worked for Carolina Power and Light doing something that involved a million tiny metal electrical gizmos that rattled around the back of his old, dented, green pickup truck. He chewed Red Man and dipped Copenhagen at the same time. And sometimes, he'd light up a smoke too.

"Mrs. Smith," Alan drawled to my mother. "Thanks for brangin' the boy out today. And may I comp-lee-mint you on your appearance today?" He bowed a little and tipped his dirty baseball cap like a Confederate gentleman.

"Oh, Alan. Really." She loved it.

It was pretty clear that Alan had never been a ballplayer himself. But that didn't stop him from hitting the best warm-up ground balls I've seen to this day. Alan Householder was the master of the fungo bat. When he hit ground balls to infielders in practice, he could place them exactly where he wanted them, like he was shooting them out of a rifle. If you've ever tried to do that, you know how hard it is. A fungo bat is longer and skinnier than a regular baseball bat. It's made to hit fly balls and grounders in practice. I've watched major league coaches who weren't as good with the fungo bat as Householder.

The whole thing happened in a flash. Alan would point at you with the end of the bat, indicating he was coming your way. Then he'd toss a baseball in front of him. It wasn't even a toss, really. He just sort of held the ball in front of himself and let go of it. And then, before the ball had a chance to fall, he'd get both hands on the handle and swing the bat with his short arms. Every swing looked the same and every swing launched the ball right at his target.

But his crowning achievement with a fungo bat came at the end of every infield practice, when it was time to hit a pop up to the catcher. All the other players were done with infield drills and had, one at a time, jogged off the field. The catcher, who all along stood next to Alan, helping the coach reload after every ground ball, had the last play to make.

And it didn't look any different than his ground balls. Alan just tilted his little body at the sky and hit a line drive — straight up in the air. The catcher always caught it. He couldn't help it. It would've hit him on the top of the head if he hadn't.

After Little League games, the whole team used to go out for milkshakes. After games on Alan's teams, we'd sit in the back of his truck and drink beer. Nothing tastes better after a hot, dusty ballgame than a Budweiser. Especially when you're 14. Alan would reach into his beat-up cooler and throw a can of Bud at each player. I'd cracked open the beer and drink it in long gulps. Big burp.

Nobody's parents found out and the team never made a big deal out of it. You never saw a bunch of 14-year-olds who could hold their Budweiser better than we did.

I played for the Swift Creek All-Stars that year and had a ball. Maybe my best year ever. Alan coached the all-star team along with another team's coach, Arch Dwyer. Arch was the hilarious divorced dad of one of our team's more troubled kids, Jeff. Arch had a brutal stutter and he sprayed spit everywhere when he talked. Where many stutterers suffer a lack of confidence, Arch seemed positively empowered by his impediment. He was without rival when it came to needling umpires. "Hey ump! Yer m-m-missin' a g-g-g-great f-f-f-f-f-f-fuckin' g-g-g-g-game!"

Every city and town in America has its legendary baseball coach. A figure who influenced hundreds of lives by teaching them the value of hard work and competition. Raleigh's baseball legend was Wiley Humphrey.

Wiley was the anti–Alan. The rangy, gray-haired man had coached Raleigh baseball teams for a thousand years and led summer teams that traveled all over the south. Half John Wooden, half Andy Griffith, Wiley never swore, never raised his voice.

Alan never said so, but you could tell he hated Wiley. I went to an open fall practice with one of Wiley's teams once. I had no intention of playing for Wiley. I just felt like playing ball that day. And anyway, fall teams were rare. On the west side of town, baseball stopped in August. That's at least two months of wasted baseball time.

I showed up for practice the way I always did: mismatched and ragged. I wore baseball pants and one of those baseball undershirts that's white with colored sleeves. I could tell Wiley wasn't impressed. He told me a couple times to tuck in my shirt during practice. Jeez, whatever. And then, though I told him my name, he insisted on calling me "the young man in the un-dah-shirt" all afternoon.

42

The other players wore full uniforms and they wore them exactly the same way. They had the same haircut, the same hitting style, said the same things to each other. Warming up, I threw a ball over someone's head and said, without even thinking, "Aw shit. My fault."

Wiley stopped warmups and demanded to know who had mussed his perfect baseball experience with such vulgarity, even though he knew it was me. I apologized and said I wouldn't do it again.

"One thing I do not tolerate on my ball teams," he said with great piety, "is vulgar language." Only, with his patrician southern drawl, when he said "vulgar," it sounded like "vulgah."

He cheered up a little, though, when he saw me take batting practice. With a huge chip on my shoulder, I ripped balls over the Needham B. Broughton High School baseball field. I had a perfect batting practice groove going that day and the ball looked as big as a balloon when it left the batting practice pitcher's hand.

We played some kind of intrasquad scrimmage that day and I don't know if I ever did make an out. I hit everything I saw. And not one guy on either team said a word to me. No "nice hit" or "way to go" or even "why don't you go away?" Nobody said anything. And I didn't say anything right back. I was obvious that, no matter what kind of day I had and no matter what Wiley thought, I wasn't going to play for this team.

Wiley gave me his phone number when the day was over and told me to call him during the week. He wanted to talk to me about a spot on his team. He said something about cleaning myself up and learning to look and act like a ballplayer.

Just to be polite, I told him I'd call him. But what I was really thinking was that I'd have to be pretty desperate to play for Wiley's bunch of dullards.

Still, I didn't want Alan to find out I'd even practiced with Wiley. I knew he'd get all weird about it.

I didn't tell him, but somebody did. The next spring, when practice started, Alan made a big deal out of it, like I was cheating on him.

"Well, ah'll be gaw-damned," he said when saw me. "Are ya sure your ol' buddy Wiley's gonna let you play with us?"

I rolled my eyes. "Aw, Alan."

"Naw, man. You wanna go play with those fuckin' robots? Go on ahead."

"C'mon, Alan. It was just a practice."

"I heard you had a pretty damn good day. I figured you was done with us. Wiley's gonna send your ass to college or some shit."

Lots of Wiley's players had gotten baseball scholarships. He had all kinds of connections to baseball programs big and small.

"Alan, it was no big deal. And I'm not going back."

Once he felt he'd exacted enough apologies and reassurances, Alan was curious about Wiley's practice. When I told him I was in the coach's doghouse before we'd finished warming up, Alan nearly fell over laughing. "See? See? That motherfucker might know everybody in the whole baseball world, every fucking scout and college coach from here to hell, but his players ain't never had any fun playing baseball. Why would you ever play if it wasn't fun?"

Raleigh was a college town. N.C. State, Duke and UNC ruled the sports page every day. Major league stories were small, wire-service accounts buried behind bylined articles about State's spring football scrimmage or Carolina's new basketball recruit. The only times the columnists wrote about anything other than college athletics was when Richard Petty did something they thought was interesting.

Things changed a little when the long-dormant Durham Bulls franchise rejoined the single-A Carolina League. While casual baseball fans in Durham, Raleigh, and Chapel Hill seemed to enjoy the Bulls, I grew to need them.

After eight uneventful years of school, I was on the verge of a rocky adolescence. My parents and I struggled to understand each other and there was a lot of yelling and crying.

I'd just spent a couple of years in a Catholic junior high school full of nuns and priests who hated kids. The stories are no different from a million Catholic school stories — fear, intimidation, creepiness.

By high school, I'd had enough. I was angry but didn't know how to express it.

So I played the role of fuck-up. I was a terrible student, failing nearly every class. I didn't know it then — and neither did anyone else — but I was paralyzed by anxiety.

The inside of my head was noisy, like a kazoo orchestra. I had trouble concentrating on school. Things I read or thought I listened closely to were gone moments later. I never showed it, but I lived in a near constant state of panic. My parents didn't understand it, my teachers didn't understand it, and I didn't understand it.

It didn't look like anything was wrong. But after a few months in high school, the troubles began.

While still a Catholic school, Cardinal Gibbons was far more tolerant of individual expression than Sacred Heart Cathedral had been. Gibbons had nuns whose hairlines peeked out from beneath their habits. Students dressed neatly, but didn't have to wear uniforms. Teachers and administrators treated kids like people.

The trouble with that was, the kids who came to Gibbons from Cathedral were like monkeys sprung from the zoo. We'd been so long in that dark, awful school with those disturbed nuns that we forgot how to go to school. If we weren't on a short leash, we had no idea how to behave. I don't really know what the girls who went to Gibbons from Cathedral did. I saw their troubles surface later. But most of the boys went nuts immediately.

Seven or eight freshmen boys who came to Gibbons from Sacred Heart Cathedral were having trouble with the tiny freedoms we were given by the Sisters of Notre Dame. The week the Cathedral boys arrived at high school, five were suspended for showing up drunk and dateless to a back-to-school dance.

I managed to avoid that evening — a death in the family took us to my parents' hometown in Pennsylvania for the weekend. But I surely would've been among the suspended had I been in town. The incidents around the dance, as well as other trouble we'd found earned us an instant reputation at Gibbons.

When I look back at high school, I realize that two things kept me from dropping out and running away. The first thing that saved me in high school was something new: punk rock. The second thing was something old: baseball.

My friends were discovering punk rock and I remember feeling like I'd had an epiphany. These kids were smart. They thought for themselves. They valued things that mattered and they ridiculed things that didn't. The music spoke directly to me. It told me not to panic. Everything would be OK. Or at least, I wasn't the only fuck-up in the world.

I think now of punk rock and how absolutely foreign it was, not just to my parents, but to my whole town. Today, the images are pretty standard. Torn clothes, weird hair, piercings here and there. But in 1981 in Raleigh, the look and the music still had the power to shock. Adults despised punk and were utterly terrified by it. No wonder it spoke to me.

Punk was important. But baseball was an anchor for my life, the only thing I still had in common with my dad, who thought my new punk rock ethos was the end of the world.

The only bond between us during my adolescence was baseball. Specifically, spring and summer evenings at Durham Athletic Park. The Bulls were good and drew consistent crowds to their ancient little ballpark wedged between tobacco warehouses and working class southern neighborhoods. After school and my own baseball practice, my dad would call me from work. "Wanna go?" That was all he'd say and I knew what he meant. It meant, get all your homework done and avoid getting into trouble before I get home. Then, we'll take a drive over to Durham, park our car and be in the $3 seats before the first pitch.

My dad and I made a funny pair at the games. On warm nights, he wore shorts and a tennis shirt and running shoes. I wore torn pants, a ratty tee shirt and filthy sneakers. My shaved head must've sparkled in the artificial light. The ballpark was the only place where none of it mattered to my dad. We were friends again. Hot dogs for dinner. Ice cream sandwiches for dessert. Talk about the game all the way home.

At Bulls games, neither of us ever brought up school troubles or the way I dressed or any of the other things that sparked arguments any place else. He told stories about his own dad and the Pirates and games he played in high school and college. And I listened and memorized them all.

I had a wallet-sized Durham Bulls schedule thumbtacked to a wall in my bedroom. I looked forward to every Bulls homestand and tried to figure out which games Dad and I would go to.

Alas, the Bulls didn't play at home every day and so my difficulties continued.

My mom and my sister went to one Bulls game a year. When the famous San Diego Chicken visited Durham Athletic Park, my whole family was there.

It was a hot ticket. The barnstorming mascot performed at a different minor league park every night and packed fans into seats wherever he went.

The Chicken crossed all kinds of barriers. Cool and square. Young and old. Fan and non-fan. The Chicken game was always the only game that sold out in advance every year. No walk-up tickets. That didn't even happen when the Bulls made the Carolina League playoffs.

He totally overshadowed the game when he was in town. He upstaged the players and the umpires, the action on the field was secondary to the mascot.

After a long Bulls game, a night where my mom and my sister laughed their heads off at the Chicken, we were among the last fans filing out of the ballpark. Behind the first base grandstand, we trudged up a ramp toward the exit, still laughing at the Chicken's goofy dances and gags. Out of nowhere, right in front of my family, the Chicken himself popped out of one of the ancient ballpark's many hidden doorways. "Hey! It's the Chicken!" my sister whooped. We stood face-to-beak with the great Chicken.

The Chicken was tiny. Maybe 5'3". And if you looked closely, you could see a person's eyes peeking out of his half-closed plastic chicken eyes. My mother addressed the Chicken, "Well, Mr. Chicken, we had a lovely evening. Thank you for coming to town." She extended her hand.

"The pleasure, I assure you madame, is mine," the Chicken said, bowing graciously and kissing the back of my mom's hand.

My mother was charmed by the Chicken. "And now I have to ask you, Mr. Chicken, I wondered all night, how do you see out of that suit?"

Suddenly the Chicken turned into Groucho Marx. "I see very well thank you. And I gotta tellya, lady, I likes what I sees!" With that, he reached around and grabbed a handful of my mother's rear end.

"Ooooh!" my mother shrieked and smacked the Chicken in the head. "Mr. Chicken!"

While high school wasn't going very well, high school baseball was.

I made the Cardinal Gibbons team as a freshman and we were loaded. I didn't play much but I bonded with the team. My teammates were curious about the rowdy Cathedral reputation. But none of the other Cathedral boys were baseball players, so I carried the mantle on the baseball team. The upper classmen got a weird thrill from the wacky hi-jinks of their freshman teammate. They'd never do those things themselves, but they loved knowing someone who did.

Skipped afternoon classes to drink beer at a nearby sandwich shop: Caught.

Hung roadkill in locker of obnoxious sophomore: Not caught.

Interrupted mid-year exams with colorful smoke bombs in the hallway: Not caught.

Made out with hottie at Valentine's Day dance: Definitely caught.

There were other incidents and the baseball team loved them all. I understand now that it's not funny for ninth graders to drink until they throw up. Or to smoke pot by themselves before team bus trips. But those kinds of things gave me instant high school cred on the baseball team. They just didn't do me any good anywhere else.

North Carolina, like most states, separates its high school athletic programs by enrollment size. Big schools play each other, medium and small schools play each other.

There weren't many schools smaller than Cardinal Gibbons. We had something like 300 kids in the whole school. Very few Catholics lived in North Carolina. Thus, very few North Carolinians sent their kids to Catholic high schools.

When anyone in Raleigh asked me where I went to school and I told them Cardinal Gibbons, they looked at me like they thought I might be kidding. "What the hell is that?" Raleigh hadn't yet become the attractive New South city that it is today. Sure, it was the state capital and was home to a major university. But in most ways, until pretty recently, Raleigh was a small, Old South town.

Public high schools in Raleigh and Wake County competed in the Capital 8 Conference. The Cap 8 pitted urban schools like Broughton and Enloe against suburban schools like Cary and Garner. The stands were usually full at Cap 8 games, no matter the sport. Game scores and conference standings were in the newspaper. The conference was easy to follow.

But Gibbons didn't play in the Cap 8. We played in a conference for tiny schools with barely enough enrollment to field a team. I'm not sure the conference had a name. But they could have called it the Miscellaneous Division for Unusually Small High Schools Within 100 Miles of One Another. We had public and private schools, schools with unbelievably rich kids and a school that was actually an orphanage. Thus, when the well-heeled old-money Episcopalians from North Raleigh's Ravenscroft visited scruffy Oxford Orphanage in the middle of the woods, the teams made an odd match. And when the Catholics from Cardinal Gibbons traveled to play our division arch rivals at the Eastern North Carolina School for the Deaf, it was hard not to feel like we were the oddball conference.

We spent a lot of time in a van and played in towns I'd never heard of. Coats, North Carolina, for example. I don't remember anything about Coats except the rock hard ballfield, covered with a blanket of pebbles. Coats had a kid named Moon Pie who hit a baseball farther than I've ever seen a non-major leaguer hit a ball.

The baseball field at Coats was without a fence and had a little slope just past where the outfielders stood. The ground rules at Coats were "all you can get," meaning pretty much everything was in play. With a field as hard as asphalt and a sloped outfield, if a ball got past the outfielders, it might roll right out of Harnett County. So, the scouting report at Coats was "play deep."

Moon Pie, who I hope has another name by now, came to the plate and jacked a long, high shot to left center field. As soon as he hit it, everyone in the rusty little ballpark knew Moon Pie had a home run.

49

But since there was no fence, he couldn't trot around the bases. He had to sprint. And sprint he did. If I didn't know better, I might actually believe I saw Moon Pie cross the plate before the ball hit the ground.

In the middle of the season, I somehow landed an actual date with the cutest girl in my class. She was quiet. She hid behind her blond hair. She was a vision in Catholic school clothes.

Nobody in school knew much about her. Meg's parents were divorced. There were rumors that she was a model, that her father moved to Paris, that she was the heir to some European fortune. She and the handful of girls she hung around with carried themselves with a world-weary dignity, like movie stars.

They chewed gum and rolled their eyes a lot. They read magazines that I didn't know you could buy in Raleigh. They always looked perfect.

Going out with Meg Huntington was like someone telling me to fly a jet. It seemed completely out of the realm of the possible. I'd dabbled in the minors; Meg was big league.

Nevertheless, my freshman sources told me that, if I were to ask Meg out, she would consent. For a week or so, I stalled and stewed, terrified, thinking up a million excuses not to ask her out.

Finally, my sources let me know the offer was not indefinite. Meg would not wait around forever.

I took the plunge. I called her on a Wednesday night.

"Say, uh, Meg. Yeah, uh... listen, I don't know if you... uh... y'know... well... maybe you'd like to go out sometime."

"Yes," she said softly into the phone. "I'd love to."

We have liftoff!

We talked for a while after that. I have no idea what we talked about. The triumphant theme music in my head was too loud to hear anything else. We made some sort of plan to see a movie on Saturday. After we hung up, I had to breathe into a bag.

Since I didn't have a driver's license, the plan depended heavily on my baseball teammate Gary Meyrl hooking me up with a ride. "Hey Gary," I said, trying to be cool. "Meg Huntington's going out with me." Gary was a senior, but had noticed the mysterious blond-haired freshman in the halls.

"Well, good for you, Romeo," Gary said. "Where you gonna take her? Chuck E Cheez?"

"Funny. Gary, man, can you do me a huge solid? Can you take me and Meg to movies Saturday?"

"No can do, Loverboy. I gotta little som'n of my own goin' on."

"Gary. I'm begging you. Don't make me beg."

"Sorry, Slick. Looks like you need a Plan B."

"Thanks for nothing."

"Yeah, well... hey, good luck Saturday, big fella."

At that moment, I should have called Meg and told her, what? Anything. Anything to get me out of this date. Why? Because Plan B involved my dad.

My father is the most unapologetically corny man in America. He's capable of embarrassing his kids from miles away. His guileless-ness can be charming. Or it can be lethal.

Alas, rather than cancel my date with Meg, I asked my dad for a ride.

"Hey dad. I'm, uh, going to the movies with a friend on Satur-day. Can you, y'know, give us a ride?"

"Sure! I don't see why not. Who's going? Matt?"

"Uh, no."

"Jerry? Dave? That Pajerski kid?"

"No, dad. You don't know her."

"HER!? Well, right on, my man!" Dad, in an effort to relate, some-times lapsed into outdated slang. "Who's the lucky gal?"

"Her name's Meg, Dad. Please promise me you won't do any-thing, y'know..."

"What?" he said, with a hurt expression. "Anything what?"

"I don't know, Dad, sometimes you act all goofy and it can be, like, embarrassing."

Dramatically, he threw his hands in the air. "Oh, I see! Your ashamed of your old dad, right?"

"No, dad. Of course not. It's just..."

"No, no! I get it, I get it. The old man's a square. A real flat tire."

"Aw, dad. Cut it out."

"Hey, if you don't want a ride on your date, that's fine with me."

"No, dad. I'm sorry. I do want a ride."

"Well, as long as you're not embarrassed to be seen with me."

I saw Meg in school and told her my father would take us to movies, a decidedly uncool turn of events. I mean, your dad could be Keith Richards and you still wouldn't want him driving you around. He's your dad, for crying out loud. She looked irritated.

"He's cool," I lied. "You'll like him."

I had a baseball game Saturday afternoon. Word had gotten around that Meg and I were going out. If a creature exists that is crueler than a high school student, it's a baseball player. And a high school baseball player is off the cruel charts. Gary the Senior led the parade.

"Fellas, I didn't believe it myself. Smitty's getting down with Meg Huntington."

"Meg? Holy shit! What, did somebody dare her?"

"Did she go blind?"

"Does she know it's a date?"

"Oh my god. It's the end of the world! Pat Smith and Meg Huntington."

On and on it went. "Stop," I said. "Yer killin' me."

But they were. As the game went on, I got more and more nervous about my date. And my dad.

Finally, after three hours of abuse from my barely human teammates, it was time.

At home, I took a shower and went a little heavy on the Old Spice, as teenage boys are prone to do. I put on every pair of pants I owned — twice — and still I looked like a dork.

I found my father in the living room, wearing bermuda shorts and reading the paper, his huge bare feet propped on a footstool.

"Dad, you ready?"

"Huh? Oh, right. Gimme a minute."

He put on a pair of shoes and we left.

Meg's house was on the north side of town. My father and I squinted at house numbers when we got to Meg's street. "There it is," I said, wishing I'd never asked her out to begin with. Such anxiety. Dad stopped the car in front of the house. Meg lived in a townhouse, with siding on it. Damn. Even her house is cool.

I opened the passenger door and started toward Meg's front steps.

"Go get 'em, big guy," my dad said.

I paused for a second and rolled my eyes.

When she answered the door, Meg looked even more stunning than she did at school. She wore tight jeans and some sort of stylish white top.

"Hi," I said. "You look great!"

"Thanks."

We walked to my father's Toyota Corolla and I opened the back passenger side door. Meg got in and I shut her door gently. While I hurried around to the other side, I could hear my father in the car, talking to Meg.

"Hi, honey! Don't you look pretty tonight!"

I didn't hear Meg say anything.

I got in the backseat behind my father and tried to think of something to say to Meg.

"So, this ought to be a good movie, huh?"

"Yes."

"What are you two going to see?" my dad asked, looking at Meg in the rearview mirror.

"E.T.," she said softly.

"Hey, wait a minute," dad said. "That's not rated R, is it? I mean, hey, that's not cool."

"Dad! No! It's PG, OK?" I was desperate for him to stop talking.

Meg stared blankly out the window. I craned my neck a little to give my father the knock-it-off signal in the mirror. He must've gotten the message. We rode in silence for an eternity.

But before we got to the movies, my dad turned on the radio. And that is when I knew I would never have another date with Meg Huntington. Elvis was on the radio.

"Hey! The King," my dad exclaimed. If my father loves anything more than baseball, it's Elvis. Unable to control himself, moved by the spirit of Elvis Presley, my father imitated Presley's vocal stylings, adding a bizarre sort of karate flourish thing with his hands.

"We're caught in a trap..."

"Oh my god. Help me," I said, my head in my hands.

"I can't walk out..."

Meg stared wide-eyed out the car window, wondering how she got involved with this maniac.

"Beeecaause I luuuuv you too much, baaaabeee!"

We finished second in the state that year, losing in the finals to a team from a town we'd never heard of. We had three seniors who would sign college scholarships. Since those guys were graduating, sophomore year was going to be my big baseball year. But I couldn't make myself pay attention to school. Getting high, meeting girls, playing ball, staying out late — who had time for school? By the second semester of the 10th grade, my grades had hit the bottom. I was failing nearly all my classes when the whole thing came down.

"Thank you all for coming this afternoon," Sister Francis said, a little too sweetly for such a somber occasion. "I know you're all very busy and could do without this hardship."

My dad wore a tie and brought a legal pad. My mother wore her white hospital laboratory uniform. They'd both left work early.

"No, no. Thank *you*, Sister," my father said, his hands folded on the yellow legal pad on the table in front of him. Though he was three or four seats away, I could see the heading written in the top margin: "Patrick: What happened?"

A parent-teacher conference for a kid like me meant that my complex world of half-truths, punk rock, marijuana smoke, and bad girls would crumble soon. Gathered around a long table, in addition to the principal and my parents, was every tenth-grade teacher at Cardinal Gibbons High School. It was January, after Christmas and before spring baseball practice. My parents knew my grades were bad, but I was pretty good at hiding exactly how bad they were. At the Cardinal Gibbons parent-teacher meeting, there was no more hiding.

Sister Francis looked at me and narrowed her eyes. "Let's get started, then." After a year and a half, she'd weeded out most of the boys from Cathedral. And now she had me in her crosshairs.

The meeting went on forever. I barely spoke. I sat at the end of the table, opposite Sister Francis. There were a couple teachers between me and my parents. My dad asked a lot of questions and was extremely polite. But the tone of the meeting was absolutely serious. My mother wept quietly throughout the proceedings.

I took a relentless pounding, as each teacher recited my sorry story.

"More than once, Patrick has arrived late to history class, smelling like smoke and looking sleepy."

Oooh. I thought she hadn't noticed that.

"Patrick hasn't handed in a biology homework assignment since September."

Wow. Has it been that long?

"Given his grades on the first three exams of the year, Patrick has virtually no chance to pass Spanish."

Yeah, but you said "virtually," right?

As the litany droned on, it became difficult to imagine what exactly I did all day at school. Once in a while, the English teacher would sneak me a sad look, like she knew how shitty it must feel to have every figure of authority in your life gathered in a room, taking turns explaining how you've failed.

"What... what on earth could be the matter?" my mother asked the group, sobbing and incredulous. "I mean, how can he be doing so badly?"

"Well, why don't we ask the guest of honor?" Sister Francis responded. "Patrick? Your mother wants to know what's the matter."

My eyes stung and my face burned as all the attention in the room swung in my direction. Slumped in my chair, I sat silent, scratching at a gouge in the blond wood table. My only goal was to endure the meeting without erupting in tears.

"Well?"

I had no answers. My father's eyes fell and he shook his head slowly.

Sister Francis was eager to get to the sentencing phase of the meeting. "So!" she said, with a little handclap that startled everyone in the room. "What are we to do?"

As if I didn't know.

My only advocate that day, and heaven knows he didn't have much to work with, was the baseball coach.

Sam Gealy understood. He didn't like it, but he appeared to understand the problems I had. Coach Gealy saw the tears in my eyes at the parent-teacher meeting. He could see me at the edge of some breaking point. He saw me sink lower and lower into shame. He knew I didn't actually want to fail all my classes. He knew something was the matter, he just didn't know what.

I don't know if it was because he cared about me or because he needed a left-handed bat in his lineup, but Gealy told the angry mob that baseball was good for me.

Sideways at the table with his legs crossed, Gealy sucked his teeth and said, "This kid's in trouble." He wrenched something from his back teeth with his pinkie. Gealy was as irritated with me and my lousy habits as anyone in the room, but understood something that no one else did. "I can see it. The worst thing we could do would be to take baseball away from him. It keeps him anchored. Without it, Patrick's liable to never make it back."

I scratched a little faster at the table.

The group rejected Gealy's recommendation, of course. You couldn't let a kid with a 0.2 grade average play ball. My grades flatlined and I never played varsity high school ball again.

The season starts tomorrow. All winter it's seemed so far away. And then, just like that, it's here. I wonder why I feel unprepared. And then I remember, it's because I am unprepared.

I've been thinking about baseball since before Christmas. I've done what I always do — bought too much baseball gear on the Internet. There's something about sending away for some kind of miracle undershirt that pulls sweat away from your body. ("Give moisture the heave ho!") As if buying new stuff can fill in for actual conditioning. Trouble is, the more of this stuff I buy, the less of it I use. I have a whole closet full of baseball crap — old jerseys, pants, worn-out socks and belts, broken bats and those things modern catchers strap to their shin guards to reduce knee strain.

But what I haven't done is get in any kind of shape. Now and then I'll go to the gym I belong to and get a sweat going. I'll lift some weights and do 20 or 30 minutes on one of those contraptions that's supposed to simulate running. And I'll feel better, healthier, more awake and alert. Then, I'll come home and eat a big bowl of spaghetti and fall asleep with a basketball game on. My brain sends me a message telling me to remain perfectly still to allow the calories and carbohydrates to affix themselves to my midsection.

But now it's time to get the uniform on and go to the ballpark. It's going to be about 50 degrees, so guys will be bundled up, I expect. I have this thing where I can't wear long sleeves when I play. I just can't hit wearing a longsleeve shirt. Neither can I hit when I'm really cold. So maybe the answer is, I just can't hit.

This year, I'm trying not to get nervous. For the past few seasons, I've gotten so comfortable with our team's once-a-week, late-night indoor workouts that I've forgotten what it's like to take the field. The practices are leisurely and we're not competing against anyone. "Hey, we're *all* winners!"

By the time the games finally start, it's a jolt. Suddenly, we're playing against other teams, teams who want to beat us. It feels rude.

Orchard Park Ballfield sits at the intersection of Baltimore's main artery and the highway ring that surrounds the city. It's in a modest suburban neighborhood, just outside the Beltway. A neighborhood recreational council sponsors the league, though few of its players actually live in the neighborhood.

When I'm catching, there have been times when I get a little hypnotized — if it's possible to get a little hypnotized — by the sound of rushing traffic on the Beltway. When the late afternoon sun bounces off the buildings past the trees on the other side of the outfield fence, the low hum of Baltimore Beltway traffic can put me in a trance. It isn't a sort of you're-getting-very-sleepy trance. It's more like a peaceful, calm feeling that I'm exactly where I'm supposed to be.

My father's mother assembled a scrapbook full of newspaper stories written about things my dad did. Box scores, game stories, photos, dramatic accounts of spelling bees. The scrapbook had a deep red leather cover that had the word "scrapbook" branded into it in a cursive typeface no one used anymore.

The book was assembled with great care. One astounding newspaper clip after another of my father's athletic heroics: burying a big jump shot or smashing a double off the wall or booting the game-winning field goal in the driving snow. You could spend a whole day reading the accounts of my dad's athletic life before I was born. The thing that struck me first, though, wasn't the huge number of clips. It was the care and love with which my grandmother collected and assembled them all. It looked like a surgeon had cut and taped and glued the stories and photos into the book. Over the years, some rough handling knocked a few things loose in the book. But overall, it was remarkable shape. It probably still is.

The book had dozens of photos tucked into little black triangles at the corners. Team photos, individual photos. People sure took a lot of photos in those days. A basketball picture of my dad at the top of an impossibly high jump to corral a rebound, protecting the ball from other would-be rebounders, the toes of his Converse All-Stars pointed at the floor. My dad and the other three players under the basket wore old style satin basketball uniforms that absorbed the entire flash from the camera. My father and these three guys after the ball leapt out of the black, like it was a stage show. The picture was completely dark, except for the four men in epic struggle.

And the struggle itself looked like paintings I'd seen in art museums. Faces were contorted from exertion, bodies twisted at weird angles, arms flailing.

I always had the same reactions in the same order when I looked through my dad's scrapbook: pride that my dad was apparently a star in and around his hometown; amazement, that his hometown paper, the Altoona Mirror, covered kids' sports as if they were the pros; and finally a great weight, that in a lifetime, I'd never have enough success of any kind to fill a scrapbook.

I wonder if my father felt the same burden. What must it have been like when his mother decided to buy a scrapbook? Did she buy it after he'd already piled up a bunch of newspaper clips? Or did she buy it before he hit those doubles and kicked those field goals? Did he feel like he had to be a small town sports hero, just to fill those blank pages?

58

Four

Before this year's over-30 opener, Joe read the lineup out loud. "Tim's pitching. Rod is at short. Scott's in center. Bam Bam, you're in left. Lance, you're at second. Alex, first base. Kevin, you're catching. Pat, third base." Apparently Abbott wasn't kidding when he told me in February that I wasn't catching this season. "You don't mind not catching, right, Smitty?" Joe asked in front of the whole team. "You want to win, don't-cha?" That's how he officially broke the news.

Thanks a lot.

Kevin O'Hare is the A's other catcher. Actually, I guess now I'm the A's "other" catcher. O'Hare's about eight inches taller than me and about 60 pounds lighter. He's a monster, built exactly like a ballplayer should be. He throws so hard and so quickly to second base that nobody dares run on him. He's got sure hands, calls a smart game and he doesn't get tired behind the plate.

Yeah, so? I'm the fucking catcher.

Catcher isn't just a position. It's an identity. The catcher is immersed in the game like no other player on the field. His job is to make the most of his pitcher's talent. If the pitcher's struggling, the catcher's got to put on a good face and encourage him. It's his job to make the pitcher believe he can get guys out, even when the catcher doesn't believe it himself. He lobbies the home plate umpire. He's sandwiched between the action and arbiter. Balls get hit inches from the catcher. There's no vantage point like it. Every at-bat is a thrill.

My grandfather was a catcher.

Bob Smith caught for neighborhood teams and teams that represented his Pennsylvania mountain town until he was into his fifties. And he wore the catcher's scars on his fingers for the rest of his life. Big knots at each knuckle. Zig-zag fingers. The three bones in each of his fingers pointed in a slightly different direction, giving his thick hands the appearance of having been disassembled and put back together wrong. The pieces all looked like they needed to be tightened a couple turns. His hands were beautiful and told a story. You could see a whole life behind the plate in those broad fingers.

I used to wonder how his fingers got so crooked. Now I know. Though I haven't played half as much baseball as my grandfather, I fear my fingers are destined to look like his. I hope so, anyway.

His brother was a pitcher. A good one, too. Frank Smith's fastball had hair on it. He got a full scholarship to Penn State. He played baseball, basketball, football and ran track. His brother Bob didn't. He stayed in Altoona and worked wherever he could find work. And he kept playing ball. He wore the flannel uniforms and the bulky sliding pads. His catcher's mitt looked more like a little couch pillow. Really, it's no wonder his hands were so gnarled. Before the days of hinged mitts, catchers had to use their meat hands to trap pitches against their mitts. Today, we crouch low and put our right hands behind our backs. We catch everything one-handed. Once, an accidental foray into old-school backstopping earned me a badly broken index finger.

Catchers in the old days didn't wear helmets, either. More than a few times, I've had a bat hit me on the top of the head when I was catching. Once in a while, a bat gets away from a hitter or someone swings too hard and the backswing conks me in the helmet. It rattles your brain around but it doesn't really hurt. You just straighten your helmet and get on with it. But imagine catching without a helmet. That backswing comes around and chops you over the head like a tomahawk and drives the little button on the top of your cap about three inches into your skull, like a thumbtack.

Bob Smith endured all of that and more. While his brother went on to the minor stardom that college athletes got, my grandfather worked hard and played ball in Altoona.

Altoona, Pennsylvania, is a baseball town again. A rust-belt city whose industrial heyday is long gone, Altoona is enjoying a minor renaissance. After decades of economic decline, the town is coming back;

what used to be old and beat up is suddenly antique and Americana. The town will never be what it once was — the industries that fueled those Pennsylvania mountain towns are gone. The railroads, the coal mines and the steel mills are open, but only at a small fraction of their capacity. A region that generations ago was full of good-paying, dependable jobs today isn't really famous for anything but the old days.

In the 1960s and early 1970s, my parents saw that opportunities were dwindling in their hometown. So in 1971, they moved our little family to North Carolina at the dawn of the New South.

Raleigh was the anti–Altoona. In the early 1970s, North Carolina's Triangle area — Raleigh, Durham and Chapel Hill — was full of promise. Prospectors from places like Pittsburgh and Buffalo and Cleveland migrated from those tired cities to white-collar and lab-coat jobs at universities and research companies in the Triangle. Today, the area has exploded with Yankees. Growing up in Raleigh, I experienced an uneasy tolerance from people whose ancestors fought under the Confederate flag. Today, old Raleigh people are pretty much resigned to sharing their neighborhoods with people who talk like the Sopranos. Hell, they even have an NHL team.

My grandparents spent a few weeks at our house in Raleigh each summer. They'd come to my ballgames and marvel at the impenetrable southern accents of people they sat next to in the bleachers. (Grandma Smith believed that Carolina accents were an affectation. Once, at a supermarket, Grandma Smith simply couldn't understand what a cashier was asking her. In the parking lot, Grandma shook her head and said, "They don't have to talk like that.") Then, they'd take me out for pizza and come back to the house and watch baseball on television until they fell asleep.

One Saturday when I was 13, my grandparents came to a double-header I was playing. My team lost the first game by a huge margin. It must've been agony to watch, because I know it was agony to play. Walk after walk in the broiling Carolina heat, my team stopped caring in about the second inning. We got our wind back in the next game and pushed our opponents to extra innings. We won on a sacrifice fly and my grandfather proclaimed the game a work of art. Exciting, dramatic, full of strategy and execution. This, after seven hours of watching 13-year-olds play baseball in the dusty summer heat.

On the way home from the game, he said, "Hey, why don't we get cleaned up and drive over to Durham to see the Bulls?"

It was OK with me and it was OK with Grandma. We rinsed off the sweat and the red dust and were in our seats in Durham in time for the first pitch. The leadoff batter for the visiting Lynchburg Mets hit a double. The next guy hit a bloop to centerfield and it looked for certain that the Bulls would trail by a run before they recorded an out. But Durham centerfielder Brett Butler — who would later have a terrific career in the big leagues — charged the bouncing ball and came up throwing. Not a smart play, probably, but the kind that's pretty common in the low minor leagues. Butler's ill-advised throw was up the third base line. The catcher had removed his mask and tossed it out of the way as soon as he saw that Butler was going to try to nail the runner at the plate. But the catcher didn't toss the mask far enough out of the way and the centerfielder's crazy throw glanced off the discarded catcher's mask in the grass and ricocheted right at the home plate umpire's head. He never saw the ball and it knocked him cold at the instant the runner crossed the plate. The ballpark buzzed while trainers from each team tried to revive the bloodied umpire, who lay sprawled on his back in the grass behind home plate, the toes of his black shoes pointing to the sky. Within a few minutes, it was clear that, while the umpire might be OK, he was in no shape to finish the game. The trainers and an EMT crew loaded the poor guy into an ambulance and took him away. A few minutes later, when the public address announcer told the crowd there would be a delay while league officials tried to find another umpire, I figured my grandparents would want to leave. Wasn't that enough bad baseball for one hot day? But before I could tell them it was OK if they wanted to go home, the PA announcer said that fans should stick around because, until the game started again, all hot dogs, nachos and beers would cost 10 cents. That was all Bob Smith needed to hear. He leapt to his feet. "Hey! How many you want?" My grandfather and I marched to one of the ballpark's ancient cinder block concession stands and ordered two bucks worth of dogs, nachos, Cokes and beers. We could barely carry it back to the seats, where Grandma Smith shrieked when she saw how much food we'd bought. But she joined right in and we stuffed ourselves with ballpark food until the new umpire arrived. We stayed all nine innings and talked about the game the whole way home.

In the mid-1990s, as Altoona's comeback was just underway, the town was awarded a team in the historic Eastern League. The Altoona Curve is the double-A affiliate of the Pirates, who play 100 miles west. The Curve's name is a play on the "Horseshoe Curve," the only thing Altoona was ever really famous for. The Horseshoe Curve is a 19th century feat of engineering that allows freight trains to hug the side of the Allegheny mountains on their way between the eastern and western parts of the commonwealth. In the days when the Pennsylvania Railroad and the Baltimore and Ohio Railroad pulled boxcars up and down the steep mountains, baseball was king. Every little burg in the mountains had a team and they all played each other. But as the towns starved, so did baseball. Sports fans in Altoona and nearby Johnstown and the tiny villages scattered across the gray Alleghenys lost interest in baseball and rooted for Penn State on Saturdays and the Steelers on Sundays. Hunting and stock car racing grew and baseball faded. The Pirates drew fewer and fewer fans every year.

But when the Blair County Ballpark was built next to a rickety wooden roller coaster just off highway 22 in Altoona, hordes of fans came to see the Curve. While minor league baseball wasn't the reason for an improved mood in and around Altoona, it was certainly part of it.

Bob Smith died in 1993, a few years before baseball returned to Altoona. They built the ballpark just over the hill from the little apartment he and my grandmother lived in. He would've loved it.

So, for my first few years in the Over-30 League, I was a catcher, like my grandfather. Last season was my best. It all came together for me, offense and defense. Well, defense more than offense. But still, I hit pretty well. And out of nowhere, I was the starting catcher on the all-star team. I had just about as good a season as I can have. I never once imagined I'd lose my catcher's job.

But I didn't say all that to Joe when he told me I wasn't a catcher anymore. I said, "Sure. Yeah. Of course I want to win."

One of the things I'll miss about not being the regular catcher is the non-verbal relationship I have with Tim Gaudet. Tim is a skinny right-handed pitcher who has a tendency to give up, shall we say, the big inning. Even when Tim is pitching well, he's liable to surrender some of the more colossal home runs you'll see in the Over-30 League.

Tim throws a fastball, a curveball and what we've come to refer to as "The Three." The first two pitches you already know about. The Three is whatever pitching motion doesn't hurt Tim's arm that day. Sometimes it's sort of a change-up. Sometimes it's sort of a slider or even a knuckleball. Most times, a catcher couldn't stand not knowing exactly what each pitch was going to do. But Tim doesn't throw hard enough for The Three to do much of anything. Except get clobbered once in a while.

When Tim endures one of those five or six run innings, it can be hard to tell if it even bothers him. His expression never changes.

Last year, late in a close game against the Browns, Tim was pitching to their most dangerous hitter, Kyle Morton, with runners on base. From behind the plate, peeking up at him through my catcher's mask, I could tell Kyle was tense. He was stepping out of the box after every pitch, adjusting his batting gloves and his helmet, stretching his neck and making weird faces by opening his eyes real wide. Down 1–2 in the count, he fouled off three or four pitches in a row.

Tim's tank was on E. He'd thrown three innings of relief already with a sore arm. His face didn't let on, but every new pitch he threw did. His elbow was hurting.

Still, he fought Kyle with everything he had. Which, by now, wasn't much.

From the stretch, Tim craned his neck a little and squinted in at me for the sign. I put down my index finger and pinkie, and tapped my right thigh, indicating that I thought Tim should throw Kyle a curveball low and outside. The anxious batter would see the ball float toward the plate and start his swing, finally lunging as the ball broke away from him and into the dirt. I'd dig the ball out of the dust and that would be all for Kyle Morton.

Tim shook his head. No. Not a curveball.

I pounded my glove and set up another sign. Index finger, wiggling. Fastball about chin high and over the plate. At best, the right-handed hitter would foul this pitch off to the first base side. High fastballs are notoriously hard for jittery hitters to hit, and nearly impossible to leave alone.

Tim shook his head. No fastball. Tim wanted to throw The Three.

I've never been a catcher who fights over pitch selection. Especially with Tim Gaudet. You're the pitcher. You're the one who's got to throw it. Tim's refusal of my first two suggestions told me he didn't think he could throw either pitch for a strike. His arm hurt too bad.

I put the sign down. OK, Tim. Three it is.

While Tim paused in his stretch to check the base runners, I quietly set myself up on the outside of the plate. I peeked at Kyle. His fingers squeezed the bat handle so hard that his batting gloves puckered. He waved the bat in a tight circle behind his head and rocked a little in the box, his hips and rear end idling back and forth. He was so wired after a long at-bat he looked like he might burst. Tim saw all this too and he wisely stood perfectly still for an extra couple seconds, just to torment Kyle. Maybe The Three was the right pitch after all.

Tim raised his left knee, pushed off with his right foot and threw his pitch.

Out of his hand, the ball was coming right to me. If Kyle swung, there was no way he'd be able to do anything with this pitch. But, as it does from time to time, The Three took a sudden turn halfway to the plate. It now moved toward the inside half of home plate, right where every catcher in the league knew Kyle liked it.

No wonder he liked it. If you can't hit this pitch, maybe you should start thinking about softball.

Kyle unloaded all of his tension, all of his tightly wrapped energy into his swing. He smashed Tim's pitch high over the left field fence for a towering three-run homer. He dropped his bat and strutted slowly around the bases, preening every step of the way.

The umpire handed me a new ball and I turned to Tim. What do you say to a pitcher after something like that? "Shake it off," I said half-heartedly.

Tim shrugged, no expression on his face at all. I'll miss that at third base.

We open against the Kings, who are awful every year. I can't tell if I like the Kings because they're such a beatable team or because they're really nice guys. Both, probably.

They lose game after game and never appear to get demoralized. A bunch of them use wooden bats and no batting gloves. Why on earth would you hit with a wooden bat when you could use one of the weapons-grade aluminum models the rest of the league hits with? Today's metal bats are so juiced they hum in your hands. Get jammed while you're hitting with one of them and you're likely to line one over the shortstop's head. Hit the same pitch off your fists with a wooden bat and it's like grabbing a live wire.

The weird thing about the Kings is they're not really bad ballplay-ers. Mostly, they're just old. The Kings are loaded with old guys and rookies who didn't know how to avoid getting drafted by a stinker. This year, though, they have a promising youngish rookie named Jay Fiore, who's also a local sportscaster. God, can you imagine the abuse that poor guy's going to get? He's rich, single, young and a total stud. And his job requires him to go to ballgames all the time. Believe me, there's not a fat, bald, working stiff in the league who wouldn't love to leave cleat marks on that fucker's chest. Or at least take enormous pleasure in any rookie mistakes he might make.

In the bottom of the first inning in the season opener, we put together a threat. Back-to-back doubles, lots of hard smashes all over the field and we were just about to blow the game open early. Then Phil LaSalle quit the team. Packed his bag and left during the first inning of the first game of the season. Phil is an affable, forty-eight-year-old night watchman who reminds you of the Maytag repair guy. He's a portly, slope-shouldered outfielder who's prone to injuries. He's been on this team for years, maybe since it started. Phil was unchar-acteristically angry at this season's playing arrangements, which were outlined in a pre-game team meeting.

Two major bombs detonated in that meeting. Bomb number one: We've decided we're going to win this year. The last couple years, Joe tells us, the reason we've stunk was because guys were playing the wrong positions. So, to remedy this, the team will pay less attention to guys' playing time and more attention to putting the best nine A's on the field as often as possible.

Bomb number two: Joe promised to control his temper this season.

Joe is the leader of the A's — for better or worse. While his step-father, DD, is listed officially as the team's manager, Joe is the team's chief strategist and motivator. Over the years, Joe's foul mouth and white hot temper have caused him — and his teammates — great trouble in the Over-30 League.

During my rookie season, Joe had one of his meltdowns on the field. He was having a lousy game and looked at a third strike to end an A's rally. It was a perfect pitch that just handcuffed him. Happens to everyone. But Joe completely lost his mind at the umpire, who must have thought he missed the call because he inexplicably didn't throw Joe out of the game for his profane tantrum. When I took my position after our half of the inning, Joe was still jawing at the umpire. It's easy to forget that cultural rules of civility can be suspended during athletic competition. If you don't like an umpire's call, you can just yell at him. I mean, you shouldn't, but you can. And you can't do it all the time, but once in a while, you can just cut loose on an umpire. And since, as the catcher, I'd spent much of the game in friendly conversation with the home plate ump, I felt bad for him. I encouraged him — quietly — to ignore Joe's silly demonstration. Warming up the pitcher as the rest of the A's took their positions, I spoke quietly to the ump, who stood just outside the left-handed batter's box, adjusting his mask. "Hey, don't sweat it," I said behind the catcher's mask. "Joe's completely out of line."

The umpire didn't say anything, likely because he knew something I didn't: Joe was standing right next to him and heard what I said.

"Goddammit, Pat! What the fuck do you know? Shut the fuck up! Stand up for your fucking teammates, you punk!" To the umpire's great delight, Joe's tantrum was now aimed at me. Is that what I should've done? Do you defend a teammate, no matter how wrong he is? Joe stomped over and stood with a foot on either side of home plate, between me and the pitcher, whose warmups had ceased. His meaty hand pulled me up by my chest protector, out of my catcher's squat. Joe pressed his face against my catcher's mask. He looked directly into my eyes. With hot breath, he whispered, *"Fuck... you... Pat."* People have said that to me before, but no one ever meant it as much as Joe did at that moment. With a little shove, he dropped me and turned around and jogged to his position.

But this year, Joe vowed in the pre-game meeting, in the interest of winning, he would keep his temper under control.

If playing time was going to be adjusted according to ability, Phil LaSalle would certainly be among the most acutely affected. He's older than most players on the team. He's thick in the middle. He's slow in the outfield. He won't throw out any base runners. He plays because he loves baseball and because he's always played it. But today, with runners on base, Phil decided to call it a career. His abrupt retirement gave the opening day win a weird feeling.

For one thing, almost nobody knew he was gone until his spot came up in the batting order. "LaSalle! You're on deck!" DD hollered.

A long pause. "LaSalle!"

"He quit," somebody hollered back.

"Quit?" DD said. "Whaddya mean, he quit?"

"He quit. He left. He's gone. Said he was sick of the whole bunch of us," Chris Nichols said, staring out at right field. He added, under his breath, "can you blame him?"

With sports on television all day and night, we're accustomed to endless replays and non-stop expert analysis. We see just about everything with our own eyes. When a player gets hurt, the cameras follow him off the field and into the clubhouse. An inning or two later, we get an update on that player's condition. And we can read further updates in the paper the next day. Fans see everything but the arthroscopic surgery.

When a player retires, he'll hold a news conference. Or at least say something to the media about it. And fans know not to look for that player again.

But when something happens in our league, it's easy to have the whole event pass without anyone knowing what happened. Imagine LaSalle's retirement if the A's-Kings game was on television. The cameras would show Phil packing up his junk in his bag. They'd follow him to his car, asking him questions the whole way. "Will you be back?" "Are you angry at DD?" "Is the team's new focus on winning good or bad for rec league baseball?" Say what you want about the media, they get answers to questions we all have.

So, instead of knowing these answers, the A's are left with a hole in the batting order and a lot of questions about why Phil left.

Winning versus fun. That's what it comes down to. Does winning equal fun? Probably, if you're one of the guys who plays all the time. But if you're sitting on the bench watching, you might just as well play a few innings and miss a cutoff man or let a grounder go under your glove. Isn't that why we all signed up? Not just to wear a uniform, but to play.

And what about the pressure on the guys who do play a lot? Is that fun, knowing that you're cutting into someone else's playing time?

Nobody's perfect, either. What happens when one of the starters drops a pop up? What do the players on the bench think? "Hell, I could've done that." My prediction: it won't take long before we see a few more Phil LaSalle-style stomp-offs.

In the late innings against the Kings, while we protected a huge lead, talk on the bench turned to Fiore.

"How did he wind up with these guys?" Kevin O'Hare asked. "There are guys on that team who could be his dad."

"I guess he just signed up to play," said Chris Nichols. "I'm sure he had no idea he'd wind up with them. He's in for a long year."

"He does a nice job on Channel 11," Abbott said, head cocked sideways, biting a hangnail. "Is he married?"

"He's on Channel 13, dumbass," Joe said. "Why? You like him? You queer for him?"

This bit of wisdom reminded me of a conversation I heard years ago, when I was a member of the grounds crew for the Baltimore Orioles. The Orioles were hopelessly behind in an early season game against Kansas City. My job that night was to sit in the Orioles bullpen with the relief pitchers. That was it. Just sit there. Open the door in the outfield wall if any of the relievers was called to enter the game. Then close the door and sit back down.

Uber-athlete and 1980s cultural icon Bo Jackson was playing left field for Kansas City. The Orioles bullpen was behind the leftfield wall. When the pitchers sat in their little wooden shed watching the game, they looked directly at the back of Bo Jackson. After some impossibly athletic catch, the pitchers, allegedly professional athletes themselves, marveled at Jackson's physique.

"Jesus, look at that guy," said doughy reliever Tom Neidenfuer. "He's a bull."

Jackson had no idea the Orioles behind him were checking him out. He kicked his foot a little at the outfield grass.

"His thighs," was all hard luck right-hander Doug Sisk could say. "God almighty! Look at his thighs."

"Can you imagine doing this and playing football too?" Mark Thurmond said. "I've never seen anyone like him. Never."

"Yeah, but I'll bet he's got a two-inch pecker," chirped Terry Kennedy. The obnoxious right-wing catcher was always good for a vulgar observation.

"No, no, no," Neidenfuer whispered, bug-eyed and with great reverence. "He's got a hammer on him. I'm sure of it."

Parties at the North Carolina State University School of Design were not for high school kids. Still, we managed to find our way in and help ourselves to the keg.

Chatting up the college girls and sneering at their sensitive boyfriends, my punk rock pals and I wore out our welcome quickly at the Design School Halloween party. Campus police rousted us away from the festivities, to the cheers of attendees who were actually invited.

Drunk and bored, we decided it was time for some creative haircuts. Really, what good was punk rock if you didn't have a weird haircut? There were many styles to choose from, and each said a little something different. The mohawk was for the fashion-conscious punk who didn't mind the maintenance. There was a haircut where you shaved everything off the back and left only the front bangs. It was a little more European than I was interested in. I went for the whole package, the total tough-guy punk rock look — the shaved head.

Today, there's nothing remarkable about a shaved head. Plenty of upstanding citizens buzz off all their hair. But in 1982, this was not the case. A shaved head meant you were a dangerous character. Or you thought so, anyway.

Most of the punk rock kids in Raleigh were the sons and daughters — mostly sons, though — of hippies who encouraged their children to express themselves. They didn't care if their kids had blue mohawks. Mine were not among those parents.

My mother regarded many of my friends as wiseasses who needed a good smack. And she was at an utter loss any time she encountered a kid with a weird haircut.

When I got home that night, my parents were already in bed. I knocked on their bedroom door and stuck my head in.

"Mom? Dad? I'm home."

"Good night, dear," my mother said, half asleep.

I figured it would be better to reveal my new hairdo here and now, rather than let them find it in the morning. "Good night," I whispered. "Oh yeah, uh, listen," I continued. "Remember how you wanted me to get a haircut?"

My mother was now wide awake.

"Turn the light on," She said quietly through clenched teeth.

"Wait, let me..."

"Turn the light on!"

I flipped the light switch.

My mother gasped. "Sweet Jesus!"

My head was like a new peach. The punk rock barber buzzed off my more-than-full head of blond hair. My big, round, white head was liberated.

"Mom, it isn't that bad!"

"Isn't that bad? It's awful! You're completely bald! What does that haircut even mean? What are you trying to do, kill me? Is that what you're trying to do?"

"No, mom. I'm not trying to kill you." I was surprised I had to hold back a laugh. Then I remembered I was drunk.

With my mother in hysterics, my father sat up in bed and shook his head.

"Come over here!" my mother barked. "Now! Get over here!"

"All right, all right! Jeez!"

"Don't you 'jeez' me, mister!"

That's how mad she was. She used "jeez" as a transitive verb and called me "mister." She wanted to inspect my freshly shorn head. She might even have shown signs of getting over it. Until I got close enough for her to smell the beer. My mother has a nose like a bloodhound. One sniff and she can tell you everywhere you've been and what you had for breakfast.

"You're drunk!"

"Mom, no. I'm not drunk."

"You are so! Donald, he's drunk! Look at him! Smell his breath!"

"Over here. Now." My dad's expression of disappointment was gone. In its place was fresh, hot anger. I walked around to his side of the bed while my mother continued hollering and asking who I'd been with and what else in God's name I had done that night.

I stood in front of my dad. He made an audible breathing sound, instructing me to breathe in his direction. What was the point? We all knew I'd been drinking. But I did it anyway.

"Hhhhhh."

The disappointed look came back. My dad frowned and shook his head. "Get out of here. Go to bed. We'll talk about this tomorrow. But believe me. You're done. No more going out. No more records. No more nothing." If you're paying attention, you noticed he didn't say anything about baseball.

The next morning was Sunday and my family was in the habit of going to 8 o'clock mass. Despite my punk rockness, I still went to mass. The Cathedral nuns had done their job; they implanted in me an irrational and obsessive fear of the smoke of hell.

The cool part about 8 o'clock mass was its dress code. Not casual, exactly. My mother called it "presentable." 10:15 and noon mass were the Catholic full metal jacket — incense, bells, organ pipes, baptisms. Jacket and tie very much required. But 8 o'clock mass was more like an early morning version of Saturday evening folk mass. Very row-the-boat-ashore. Plus, it was way shorter than the other Sunday masses.

So, despite a headache you can only get from too much Schaefer beer from a keg, my newly liberated scalp and I got ready for church early the next day. I put on some jeans and the same black jacket I always wore. I peeked at my bald head in the mirror and told myself I looked pretty damn cool. "The shaved head. The jacket. You badass. That's some punk rock, right there. Nobody's messin' with you." I gave myself a wink in mirror and emerged from my bedroom. I pulled a half gallon of orange juice out of the refrigerator and took a long pull from the paper spout on the carton.

"No!" My mother appeared out of nowhere, exploding from behind the refrigerator door. She yanked the carton away from my lips, splattering a stream of sticky orange juice down the front of my jacket. "You're not leaving this house looking like that." I wondered if this meant I wasn't going to mass with my family. This might work out OK after all. "You march back into that room and dress like an American."

"What's that supposed to mean?" I asked. "An American?"

"Just go!"

"No, really. What do you mean by that?"

"What do *I* mean? What do *you* mean? What in the hell does that haircut mean? Get out of my sight and change your clothes! Fast!"

When I returned to my room to take another stab at getting dressed for church, I started wishing maybe I hadn't shaved *all* my hair off. It turns out, when you dress for church with a freshly bald head, you don't look tough or punk rock. You just look like a weirdo. I put on a pair of dress pants and a button-down shirt. Totally over-dressed for 8 o'clock mass, but this was no longer about church. This was punitive.

Sure enough, all eyes were on me when we walked into the big marble church. C'mon, people! Never seen a bald head before? Eight o'clock mass was one of the longest hours of my life.

Before the game today, while the A's were taking batting practice, Scott Abbott coasted his pickup truck into the dirt parking lot up the

73

hill from the ballfield. Customary for Scott, he emerged from his truck wearing gym shorts and a tee shirt with the sleeves cut off. Today, though, he had with him a woman who looked like she might have, hours earlier, been sliding up and down a shiny pole with dollar bills sticking out of her underwear.

"Whoa," Stu Stoffer said, looking up the hill at Scott's date. "Who's Scotty's new friend?"

The rest of the A's tried to be cooler than Stoffer when they peeked at Abbott's companion. Kevin O'Hare glanced up the hill and mumbled, "Somebody forgot to tell her this is the washed-up league."

The new girl made her way confidently down the hill while Scott put on his uniform behind his truck.

If it's possible to overdressed and underdressed at the same time, Scott's new girlfriend was both. Between her too-small tee shirt and her tight shorts was a stripe of hypertanned flesh, punctuated by a tiny silver ring through the top of her navel. She was short and thin, and her enhanced breasts were trained to move only when she did. She wore plastic sandals that showed off her perfectly painted red toenails.

Once down the hill, she addressed the suddenly silent A's.

"Hi, guys."

"Well, hello there, sweetheart," Stoffer gushed, almost before she was done greeting us. He strolled over to Abbott's date. "What's your name?"

"I'm Candace," she said. "I'm here with Scott."

"Candace, huh?" Stoffer oozed. "Does anybody call you Candy? Because — "

Joe cut him off before he could finish. "Stu, shut up. You're embarrassing yourself."

Stu, who's actually incapable of embarrassment, was undaunted. For the rest of the day, he never strayed far from Candace. While I was in the batting cage, she and Stu stood chatting behind me.

"I'm a massage therapist," Candace told Stu. "Back home in Florida."

"Oh man. I have this thing right here in my neck," Stu said, wincing and lifting an arm over his head. "Christ, it's killing me." He lolled his head around, clutching the base of his neck.

"Here. Let me help you with that," she told Stu, reaching for his neck. In one motion, he was in the grass and she was behind him, kneading his shoulders and neck, while he groaned with pleasure.

Abbott, now in full uniform, walked past them. "I see you guys have met Candace," he said.

"Yeah, where'd she come from?" DD asked.

"I met her at Orioles Fantasy Camp in Florida."

"A massage therapist with a rack like that," Lance said. "That's fantasy camp, alright."

We beat the Pilots 12–7 today. But it wasn't nearly that close. They scored five runs in the last inning, long after we'd stopped caring. They got their runs off Tim Gaudet.

By accident, we wound up at the bar with the Pilots after today's game. We have an ugly history with them. Especially Alex.

Two years ago, the A's were pounding the Pilots in a mid-season game between two teams going nowhere. Bill Surkowicz, the Pilots' pitcher, is a short, skinny lefthander with a big mouth and a straight-as-a-string fastball. Ahead 9–0 in the sixth inning, the A's had the bases loaded with nobody out. Surkowicz's first pitch hit Alex right in the neck, below the ear flap on his batting helmet. Alex didn't fall over in pain or even grab his neck. Silently, he dropped his bat and took two steps toward the mound. A few chuckles from each bench. Frequently, when a player gets hit by a pitch, there's some clowning around between the batter and the pitcher, just to show there are no hard feelings.

But after Alex's second step, he surprised both teams with a full sprint toward the pitcher's mound.

"Aaaaa! Get away from me, you fucking freak!" the terrified pitcher shrieked in a cracking, high-pitched voice. Alex continued his charge and grabbed the pitcher by the back of his shirt. Surkowicz curled up and tried to shield his head and body from Alex, who landed three quick punches to the pitcher's ear. Both teams poured onto the infield hollering and pushing and shoving. A pile of swearing A's and Pilots formed behind the mound, Surkowicz and Alex at the bottom. Those of us who were late arriving to the scene tried to figure out what we should do. Jump on the pile? Start a new one? Try to break it up?

75

The Baseball Code says if your teammate is engaged in a fight, you join him as quickly as you can. But was Surkowicz really throwing at Alex? With the bases loaded, behind by nine runs? It seems pretty unlikely. And I started feeling bad for Surkowicz, who was sure to earn a reputation around the league as a First-Class Spazz after his shrill, squealing matador performance as Alex barreled at him like an angry bull.

As the rest of us groped and tugged disingenuously at each other, the little pitcher somehow squirted out of the bottom of the dog pile. His hat was gone, his shirt was almost sideways and he looked like he was crying. There were seven or eight of us between him and Alex, who still silently stalked the guy.

After a long suspension, Alex returned to the team, still convinced that little Surkowicz was throwing at him. There's still an uneasiness between the teams and league legend says the A's won the fight. Pilots players are still really quick to apologize for hard slides or inside pitches. We have them spooked. When anything happens, they put both palms up and say "Hey, hey, now. It's cool. Just an accident. Don't get excited."

In other news, as I learn my new position, I've forgotten how to hit. I took an oh-fer in game one. And another in game two.

Going hitless in the first game of the season made me a little nervous. It crossed my mind that, ha ha, I might never get a hit. Maybe, ha ha ha, I won't get a hit all year.

And then when I didn't get a hit in the second game either, the feeling went beyond nerves. Aw shit. Maybe I really won't ever get another hit. And the more I thought about it, the worse it got. I hit something like four straight ground balls right to the second baseman over the course of those two games. Sandwich those grounders between some strikeouts and pop-ups and you're looking at the makings of an early season slump.

Throughout this mini-slump, I have to remind myself that I'm actually a good contact hitter. I have quick hands and I don't strike out much. When you're in a slump, that's easy to forget. I've felt completely lost at the plate for the first two games. And to make things worse, I play on a team full of hitting coaches. Stay inside the ball. You're pulling your head out. Trust your hands. Even if I knew what these expressions meant, I wouldn't pay attention to them. Tune them all out and rely on your instincts. Sooner or later, you'll come around. Right?

We're 2–0. The A's are doing everything right. The team's hitting, pitching, fielding — everything. And they're having a great time doing it. And I'm miserable. I never really thought changing positions would be such a big deal.

The Pilots threw two lefthanders at us. As a left-handed batter, some of my scariest moments in the game have come against left-handed pitchers. The pitched ball appears to originate behind me, from a point beyond my field of vision. I have to open my batting stance slightly to see the ball properly. Left-handed pitchers who are adept at exploiting their advantage over left-handed hitters will even toe the pitching rubber closer to the first base side, just to get that extra few inches. The bastards.

Lefthanders who throw me breaking pitches should ask their wives to bring video cameras to the games. It would be a shame not to preserve the comedy. If a pitcher throws me 10 curveballs from his left hand, he will enjoy the exact same scene 10 consecutive times. The ball appears headed for my upper body, my head even. Naturally, instinctively, rationally, my knees buckle, I tuck my head behind my shoulder and wait for the ball to hit me in the ribs.

The ball, of course, does not hit me in the ribs. It hits the catcher's mitt. The umpire, barely able to contain himself, bellows "Stee-ri-i-i-i-ke!"

Against the Pilots, I twice grounded out to the second baseman, struck out and walked. And the walk was borderline.

Struggles and self-doubt in a slump are bad enough. But I've never seen a slumping ballplayer who wasn't also confounded by fate. The hardest ball you've hit in weeks goes right in the pitcher's glove. A sure double down the line turns into a double play because the first baseman is holding a runner.

And that's what makes me nervous. None of my at bats have been close. I haven't hit a ball hard yet. If I don't break out of this soon, I'll start hitting the ball hard and getting robbed. How many times have you heard it? "Aw, tough break. You can't hit it any harder than that." That's baseball code for, "Dude, give it up. You have no chance."

Five

====================

Every team in the league has at least one jackass. He's the guy who tries to put down a bunt with an eight-run lead. And he's the guy who drops a pop up and blames somebody else. And he's the guy who doesn't help put the equipment away after the game.

Our jackass is CJ Demakis.

The son of perhaps the wealthiest man in Baltimore, CJ drives a convertible Jag to the games and is a prostheletizing born again Christian. Of course, his faith doesn't prevent him from yelling at his teammates when they make a mistake or from whining at the umpires.

If CJ knows he's the team jackass, it's not apparent. He takes merciless abuse from nearly all his teammates and doesn't even seem to know it. If he wasn't so obnoxious, I'd feel sorry for him.

CJ probably encounters it everywhere he goes, but his baseball teammates are the only ones who actually tell him they resent his spectacular wealth. CJ's father, a Greek-American, self-made ultra millionaire who started after World War II with one bakery, today owns just about everything in East Baltimore. He grew up hard in ethnic Baltimore and, like so many immigrants, when he became successful, gave his kids everything he didn't have. And lots more. "The first thing CJ does when he wakes up in the morning," Joe says loud enough for the whole team to hear, "is check his driver's license to make sure his last name's still 'Demakis.'"

The A's are brutal to CJ and he deserves every hassle, every jibe he hears.

Today, CJ managed to get picked off first base and drop a line drive hit right to him at second. Still, when I bobbled a ground ball at third and threw too late to get the runner, CJ yelled at me from second base. "Come on, Pat! Get in the game! We can't afford mistakes like that!"

I told him to shut up, as did the rest of the infield, our manager and the base umpire. When the inning was over, I confronted him on the bench.

"CJ, if you have something to say to me, you need to say it one to one," I told him. "Not on the field. You may not fucking show me up. Ever. I mean it."

"Hey, I'm not trying to show you up," CJ said. "You gotta make that play." Arguing with CJ is useless. If you're not committed to beating the hell out of him, there's no sense arguing. I wasn't, so I told called him a dumbass and walked away.

There's an unwritten rule at every level of baseball forbidding players, managers and umpires from "showing up" one another. To show up someone, you have to do something that makes them look silly at a moment when they're most vulnerable. After an error, for example, teammates of the player who committed the error should quietly encourage that player. They should not throw their hands in the air or make any exclamations about that player's skill, as CJ does.

Umpires are particularly sensitive to being shown up. A player can debate a call. But the moment he becomes theatrical about it, he risks the umpire's wrath. You can say just about anything to an umpire — again, just about — as long as no one out of earshot can tell there's a dispute.

Bam Bam Goodrich got tossed from a game late last season for showing up an umpire. After two called strikes that Bam Bam thought were inside, he stepped out of the box and told the umpire he'd missed both calls. He spoke with his head down, kicking dirt around the outside of the batter's box, to avoid showing up the umpire. The home plate umpire, a hothead named Dave who's got an answer for everything, disagreed. Both pitches caught the inside corner, Dave said. Then he told Bam Bam he didn't care to hear any more from him. That's when Bam Bam got angry. He'd followed the unwritten rules and kept his head down when he complained. He hadn't waved his hands around or yelled in the ump's face. He figured he was entitled to a little slack.

"Hey, take it easy, Blue," Bam Bam said, employing the universal nickname for umpires. "I'm just telling you you missed a call."

"And I'm telling you to get your ass back in that batter's box and play ball!"

"I need a little time to regroup after those inside strikes you called on me," Bam Bam said, looking directly at Dave.

"There was nothing wrong with those pitches! They both got the inside corner!"

"No, no, see..." Bam Bam said. "Here's the inside corner." He reached across the box and used the bat to draw a line in the dirt to demonstrate where an inside strike might be.

Dave the umpire snapped. "You're outta the game!" He ripped his mask off and gave an exaggerated heaving motion to let the whole world know that Bam Bam was tossed. "You may not draw a line in my batter's box! I won't take that shit from anybody! Now get out of here! Now!"

Bam Bam was incredulous. He dropped the bat and stood at home plate, looking at the A's bench with his palms in the air.

"Out! Get out before you're suspended. Get the hell out of here!"

Bam Bam knew he was defeated and that any more discussion would likely cost him a game or two. Still, as he walked toward the bench, he looked over his shoulder and said, "Hey Dave."

The umpire, adjusting his lineup card so that it would no longer include the surname "Goodrich," looked up.

"You suck."

While a player only needs to be 30 to play in our league, most players are between 35 and 45.

Every season, as I get a little slower, I'm grateful for the rules concessions the Over-30 League makes. The rules are there to democratize the game, making sure that everyone gets a chance to play. But they're also reminders that no one in the Over-30 League is as good as they were when they were 18.

For example, the batting order includes as many players as have shown up that day, rather than just the nine guys in the game at any given time. If you're hot or tired, you can sit out an inning or two and still return to the game. Pitchers can't throw more than four innings. The rules are designed to make sure everybody plays at least a few innings. In my first season or two in the league, I thought the rules were silly and were costing me innings. Now I'm happy to have an excuse to take a rest.

The sorrier Alex Bell feels for himself, the better he hits.

In the 1960s, Alex was a farmhand in the Orioles system. He spent three or four seasons in Bluefield, West Virginia, playing pro ball and earning a reputation as a maverick and a bigmouth, a reputation he cherishes to this day.

Ask Alex what happened to his professional baseball career and he'll tell you: Everyone thought he was a prick. Everyone. His manager, his teammates, the umpires, the other teams. They all hated him. Alex recounts, with no small amount of pride, the numerous times he defied orders from his manager and from the Orioles minor league officials. They can't tell me what to do, he told himself. And them.

Alex was a hard throwing left-handed pitcher with control issues to match his anger issues. If he'd been a third-baseman or even a right-handed pitcher, the Orioles would have packed his bags for him after a week of training camp.

Instead, because he threw with his left hand — and he threw very, very hard — the Orioles made a mild commitment to break their young stallion. When pitching coaches tried to smooth out his choppy delivery, he'd tell them to shit in their hats. When batters crowded the plate, Alex's precious home plate, he'd throw at their heads.

Alex fought and fought dirty. Nothing was off limits. Balls, hair, eyes — if Alex was in a fight with you, his goal was injury. The more severe, the better.

Naturally, after three seasons, the Orioles tired of Alex's childishness and released him. The Pirates or the Mets or Cincinnati gave him a brief shot on one of their low minor league teams. But Alex's reputation was pretty well known, and when his new team let him go, that was that.

But he never stopped playing. Unlike nearly everyone in the Over-30 League, Alex never took a break from baseball. He played every year on two or three different teams. Even today, in addition to the Over-30 League, Alex plays in the Over-40 League and, incredibly, the Over-18 League. In 1969, he joined a team in that league. He's played every year since.

In the winter before each season, the A's get together a couple times at an indoor batting cage. In addition to pitching machines that sling hard rubber balls at varying speeds, this particular facility features a big, plywood pitcher's mound and a batting tunnel. Players can hit off real pitching, which is preferable to hitting off a machine any day. Unless the pitcher is Alex Bell.

In January and February, players come to the workouts just hoping to get their swings back. Pitchers take it real easy throwing off the mound. Strictly loosening sessions. Except for Alex, who knocks his teammates down when they crowd the plate.

At one of our winter workouts last season, I found myself standing in the batter's box, looking up at Alex on the mound. Since I bat left-handed, I prefer to hit off right-handers, especially before the season starts. I'm just looking to hit a few balls hard. But we were short of pitchers and I imagined it might be good for me to start the season with a challenge.

Since batting practice isn't particularly dangerous, no one wears a helmet when he hits. I took a few practice swings before I set my feet and indicated to Alex I was ready. He wound up and whizzed a tailing fastball right at my chin. I dropped to the floor, just underneath the pitch. Now, in batting practice — and sometimes even in games — when a ball gets away from a pitcher and throws a scare into a batter, the pitcher lets the batter know he's sorry. He'll say something like, "Hey, it slipped," or "My fault. You OK?" Not Alex. He turned his back and got a another ball from the ball cart. I got up, brushed off my pants and got ready for a pitch to hit. Alex wound up and uncorked a pitch even scarier than the first. Again, I flopped to the floor, ducking the bullet that Alex fired at my head.

Now I was mad. "Hey! What the fuck? Take it easy, Alex! Just throw me a fucking pitch to hit!"

"Get back in there," he said derisively. "I'm not gonna hit you."

Alex had no reason to throw at me. And he really had no reason

83

to throw at my head. We always got along OK. Now, though, I wasn't so sure.

Without a helmet, I was a little scared to step back in. But I didn't want Alex to know he'd rattled me. So I tapped the fake home plate and waved my bat slowly, determined not to bail out.

But sure enough, the next pitch was a heater, up and in. I leaned backwards, tensed up for the impact as the ball bore in on me. It glanced off the pinkie knuckle on my right hand and shot into the batting net.

"Ow! Goddammit Alex!" I was on one knee, holding my bruised hand. "If you can't throw a strike, get off the mound!"

"Who can't throw a strike?" Alex hollered. "You think I can't throw a strike? You were crowding the plate!"

"Alex, it's batting practice, you fucking psycho! What's the matter with you?"

"It's pitching practice, too. I'm not gonna just stand here and let you get a hit off me."

Alex is nearly 60 years old. Built like a weathered all-day sucker, Alex has gnarled, skinny legs and a gut that pokes straight out. At the beginning of this season, I sat in the right field grass before a game, stretching next to Alex. He was having trouble putting his shoes on. His belly was in the way. "I put on 20 pounds over the winter," Alex lamented. "It's been a good ride, but this is my last year."

Alex has sadly declared each of the past four seasons his last. When I point out that his talk of retirement has become an annual tradition, Alex ignores me and continues concentrating on his shoe.

Another win today, another hitless day for me. Yay.

Today, nothing was close. Dinky ground balls, one after another. I did put down a nice bunt, though. Bunting's something I take great pride in.

We were down 3–1 to the Browns in the third inning. Joe singled. Lance Blake walked. The way I've been hitting — and with my slow feet — I'm a perfect candidate to hit into a rally killing double play. Or, as slow as those two baserunners are, a triple play, even. Wisely, DD gives me the bunt sign. Usually, I can get a bunt down on the first try, no matter where the pitch is. This time, my first bunt attempt rolls

84

slowly foul over the third base line. Crap. Now, they know the bunt is on. They'll play the corners in, making it harder for me to advance the runners, both of whom are nearly as slow as I am. Nearly.

Bunting is a funny thing. As soon as you square around, the infielders suddenly begin moving in all directions. It can be difficult to pay attention to the ball, with all that motion swirling around. For a left-handed batter, bunting means keeping the right hand down at the bat handle and the left hand up at middle, just below the barrel. Hold the bat real loose, to deaden the ball's momentum when it meets the bat. If you squeeze the bat, especially an aluminum bat, you'll hit the ball too hard. But most important of all, do not get beneath the ball with the bat. A successful bunt requires the bunter to adjust his definition of success. That's hard enough to do. But a popped up bunt feels worse than 10 strikeouts. Admit it. You've said it yourself when a player has popped up a bunt: "Jeez! He can't even do THAT right." When you screw up a bunt, you bear the weight of every television or radio announcer who laments the lost art of moving runners over. You haven't just failed. You've let down your ancestors. You feel like the symbol of everything that's wrong with baseball today.

So, as the ball comes in, split it into two halves, an upper and a lower. Touch the slack bat to the upper half of the ball and you've put down a good bunt.

This time, I laid down a perfect bunt: toward third base, but past the pitcher. The third baseman had to rush in a few steps to field the ball, while Joe ran easily behind him to third. I was out by 10 feet at first base, but it felt good when the next batter grounded a single up the middle to score both runners.

The once-proud Browns are struggling for the first time since I joined the league. But for a team that takes things so seriously, the Browns look like slobs.

The Browns are the only team in the league with totally mismatched uniforms. They look like little leaguers. Most of them wear St. Louis Browns tee shirts and rumpled old red hats. I feel bad for the guys on that team, because the uniforms are one of the best parts of the Over-30 League.

Except for the Cards, teams wear big league uniforms. If you haven't worn a baseball uniform in a long time, you should try it. It feels great. And unlike the clothes you wear to work, the pants, the shirt, the socks — they already match! Be prepared, though — your wife will call it a "costume" or an "outfit."

Remember one very important rule. When you put on your uniform, you will be tempted, even compelled, to look at yourself in a mirror. At all costs, avoid this temptation. You will, if you're anything like me, feel ridiculous. You'll think very hard about leaving the house looking like that. When you put the uniform on, especially a big-league style uniform, you'll feel transformed. When you see yourself in that uniform, you'll remember that you have, in fact, not been transformed.

The hardest part — literally — of wearing a baseball uniform for the first time in years is the cup. Every other part of the game has enjoyed amazing technological advances since the last time you played. The bats are made of weird space-age metal. Shoes are more comfortable than your bedroom slippers. You can buy 50 different kinds of batting gloves. But cups are essentially the same crude piece of equipment as they were in Abner Doubleday's era. Or Socrates' era, for that matter.

A cup is a triangular piece of plastic designed to protect your nuts. And, by and large, it does. But in the process, it causes all sorts of other problems.

If you've never worn a cup, you cannot possibly know how awful it feels before you get used to it. They're plastic and ventilated and they fit — sort of— in a pouch on the front of your jock. The first time I ever saw a cup, I didn't know which end was the top and which was the bottom. It seems backwards. It doesn't make sense that you get all gathered up at the pointy end at the bottom, wasting all that roomy space at the top. I don't know. Maybe I'm doing it wrong.

Everything went our way today.

"Claire! Claire!" yells Stu Stoffer from the first base coach's box. Kevin O'Hare, the runner at second, glances at him perplexed from under an ill-fitting plastic green helmet. "Claire!"

In our league, there are no designated base coaches. Just players whose turns at bat are far enough away that, to stay involved in the game stand in the coach's boxes next to first and third.

Stu's feet are shoulder length apart. As he stands next to first base, he leans forward, bent over a little at the waist. His hands are cupped over his mouth like a bullhorn and Stu's already piercing voice is amplified even louder. Staccato, desperate bursts of "Claire!" pepper the field. The defense is confused. So is the base runner. "Claire!"

"Who the fuck is Claire?" Lance Blake asks me. We're sitting next to one another on the bench, spitting sunflower seed shells at the fence that protects the bench from foul balls.

"He's not saying 'Claire,'" I explain to Lance. "He's saying 'clear.' Like 'the coast is clear.' The shortstop's not sneaking up behind him. He means Kevin should get a bigger lead."

Lance's new, but not shy. He already hates Stu, a pain-in-the-ass .160 hitter who offers counsel unsolicited. "Move your hands up a little in your stance," Stu told me a few weeks ago. "Throw your hands at the ball. You're doin' it all wrong. Look! Your weight's all on your front foot. I'll tellya right now, buddy, you're never going to get a hit like that. You might as well just give the fuck up right now."

But right now, at this moment, Stu's job is to keep O'Hare from getting picked off second base.

"Claire!"

The pitcher, the second baseman and the shortstop clearly — or Clairely, in this case — think Stu is speaking in some kind of code. They believe the A's have some cleverly disguised scheme to move Kevin to third base. Is it a bunt? A hit and run? Will he try to steal third? What does "Claire" mean? Maybe if Stu were hollering "Mary!" or "Emma!" the A's would have a different play on. The infielders think that, like a football quarterback calling an audible at the line of scrimmage, the A's are changing their complex base-running strategy right in the middle of the game. In fact, the first base coach just talks funny.

The pitcher attempts a pickoff from his stretch. He whirls around and fires the ball to second. Kevin, flatfooted and paying more attention to Claire than to the pitcher, is 15 feet from the bag. The ball easily beats him to second, but no one's there to catch it. It flies on a straight line directly over the base and settles into the outfield grass while the centerfielder charges in to pick it up. O'Hare, looking over his shoulder, jogs to third.

From the bench, we cheer Kevin and hoot at the pitcher.

"That's the dumbest thing I've ever seen," Lance proclaims, shaking his head.

Six

Another one-sided win, this time over the Tigers and this time, I get two hits. Now we're getting somewhere.

In some ways, I don't blame Abbott for joining the Tigers last year. They're a classy team. Even now, when they're losing, there's something dignified about them. They're sharp looking. They have clear leadership. And they don't let their kids run around the bench.

Playing for the A's is like Romper Room, only with swearing. Kids of all ages roam the benches, running around, asking questions, digging in your bag, drinking Gatorade out of your cooler. I don't have kids. Maybe this is cute and I'm just missing it.

But it's not complete anarchy; there are unspoken team rules about bringing kids to A's games. The cardinal rule is this: Kids will not affect players' language. On the A's, baseball without swearing isn't baseball at all.

Three little boys sat at the end of the A's bench today. None of them was older than about seven. Gary "Bam Bam" Goodrich, after being called out on strikes threw a batting helmet that ricocheted around the bench like a bullet in the old west. "MotherFUCKer," Goodrich exploded, right next to the big-eyed boys, who watched silently, feet in their little sneakers dangling off the bench. Bam Bam sat right next to them and unfurled a string of obscenities at the home plate umpire so impressive that the rest of us could only admire it. "That's the fucked-uppenest horseshit call in the history of this stupid fucking game! You ree-DIC-u-lous JACKoff!" It went on. Scatology, anatomy, reproduction and blasphemy were each well-represented in Bam Bam's tantrum. Each of the little boys had that look kids get when they're learning something, absorbing a new experience. Not afraid or

89

offended. Fascinated. You could tell this was one of those moments they'll remember for a long time. It'll come up later. "Mrs. Martin, this is the fucked-uppenest homework assignment in the history of this stupid fucking school!"

We played a perfect baseball game today. We pitched smart. We played good defense. We hit cutoff men. By not swinging at bad pitches, our hitters forced the Tigers to throw strikes.

I led off the second inning and I swung at the first pitch in my first at-bat of the game, a fastball moving across the plate. My swing felt good and I hit the ball hard over the second baseman's head. The outfield grass slowed the ball down, so the right fielder had no trouble getting to it. That's fine. I'm not greedy. A solid single and I'm back in business.

On the bases, I'm what's known as a station-to-station guy. The ball's got to be hit a long way for me to advance more than one base. Twenty years and 80 pounds ago, I used to be a pretty fast runner. That's before I started eating french fries and corned beef sandwiches for lunch behind a desk.

Anyway, like I said, I'm not greedy. A solid hit, a good day in the field — and another win, of course — were enough for me. But suddenly, I was sent a divine sign that my slump might be ending: I got a break.

In my third at-bat of the day, I was behind one ball and two strikes. One reason I don't strike out much is, with two strikes, I choke way up on the bat. My goal changes from hitting the ball hard somewhere to merely putting the ball in play. Especially in a lopsided count, I crowd the plate and, choke up ready to swing if the ball's even remotely close. I get knocked down a lot this way, and once in a while the ball hits me in the back. That's OK. Whatever it takes.

In this at bat, the pitcher threw me a curveball on the outside part of the plate. It may have been a ball, but it was too close to take. I swung my shortened swing and the ball hit off the end of my bat. Poked the opposite way, the ball took a crazy bounce and eluded the third baseman. The gods smiled and it will, as they say, look like a line drive in the box score.

At some point during my little hitting spree, I had to slide and I got a strawberry on my ass. When you're 18, sliding is a natural thing. When you're older, it's, um, not. Even after four years in the Over-30 League, sliding's not instinctive or natural. And when you slide tentatively, you get a strawberry.

Mm-mm! Delicious! Who doesn't love a strawberry?

It might seem like a strawberry is just an abrasion. While it is, technically, an abrasion, it's hardly "just" an abrasion. It's an abrasion caked with dirt and gravel that will never find its way entirely out of your wound.

Strawberries happen when players slide badly. Rather than a smooth slide that starts low to the ground, an upright baserunner throws a leg in front of himself and tucks the other leg under. The first part of a sliding player to scrape the ground is either his knee or his ass. Either way, if the slide's not smooth, you're in for a 'berry.

Dragging a piece of flesh across hard dirt is a uniquely painful endeavor. The initial sting brings hot tears to your eyes and it lasts longer than you think it will. And the only thing more painful than getting a strawberry is cleaning one. Which means, you don't clean them. Thus, almost as a rule, they become infected.

In high school, I had infected strawberries for months at a time. At some point, I played in some kind of pre-season practice game for a team named after an insurance company. I scalded a line drive to right center field and knew it'd be good for at least a double. Out of the box, I flew around first base, but made too wide a turn after I hit the bag. The right fielder backhanded the ball on the second bounce. He spun around and made a perfect throw to second. What should have been a standup double became a close play. I slid to the inside part of the base to avoid the shortstop's slap tag. I only knew how to slide on my right leg, so I had to slide toward left field and grab the base with my right hand. I just did beat the throw, but the slide tore open both the knee of my pants and my knee itself.

I stood up right away and smacked the dust out of my pants, producing a thick brown cloud. My knee stung so bad I was woozy, but I didn't let on. It was only a scrape, but God almighty it hurt. When I bent over discreetly to inspect the damage, my right pantleg opened like a flap on an Advent calendar. Only instead of a candle or a wreath, out popped a four or five-inch abrasion that looked like raw meat. Blood streamed down my shin and into my sock.

The next guy made an out, stranding me at second. I jogged to the bench without bending my leg and threw on the catcher's equipment. When I strapped the shin guard tight against my bloody knee, I let out a quick gasp. It felt like a fire in my leg. In just the few minutes since I'd flayed it, the bleeding stopped and my knee swelled. I walked stiff-legged to my position and kicked at the ground for a second, knowing that when I squatted down, the wound would open up again. I took a deep breath and bent both knees. Mother of God.

By the time I got home, my leg looked like it might need to come off, an ugly mix of blood and dirt. The strawberry radiated an angry heat. My mother wanted to clean it, a good idea considering how much dirt the wound held. But even the slightest touch was unbearable. Mom had ideas about alcohol or some kind of anti-bacterial. And scrubbing. She wanted to scrub the already raw strawberry. Scrub it real hard.

I refused to let my mother or anyone else near my open wound and, in time, the strawberry took on a life all its own. It became a culture, a teeming, infected city on my kneecap, overrun with filth and germs. It grew. It throbbed. It wept. It cracked and bled.

A few years before, my father had a similar sliding injury in a softball game, only his strawberry was on his ankle. (Jeez, Dad. Nice slide.) Like mine, his had gotten infected, caked with infield dirt. But he made the mistake of listening to my mother. After a couple of days, he went to a doctor. The only thing I know about what happened next involves two words: wire brush. No doctors for me.

The awful strawberry threatened to keep me home from summer school. But so that I wouldn't have to miss a precious day of geometry in July, my mother fashioned a knee bandage out of women's sanitary products. I had no idea what these strangely shaped — and super absorbent! — little bandages were, in their little pink baggies. But they had sticky bits on the back and did seem to work. But by lunchtime, my oozing knee had soaked the homemade bandage, which now seemed to weigh about six pounds.

That evening, when my mother got home from work, I told her I knew it was time to do something about the strawberry. I was sweating. "I feel sick, Mom." She gently told me to get in the bathtub, but not to run any water in it. I sat in the tub in my underwear with my head back, feeling feverish against the cold bathroom tile. Mom came in and went to work. A bottle of peroxide, a toothbrush, a bar of soap and a washcloth. It may as well have been a belt sander, rock salt and a blowtorch. The more she scrubbed the furious, hissing wound, the more dirt — I mean real dirt, like from the ground — came out of it. Red dirt, from the Raleigh Optimist Park infield. It was a wonder there was any infield left at all. Peroxide, scrubbing, soap, more scrubbing, more peroxide. And screaming. Lots of screaming.

No one can complain about the job Kevin's doing as the A's starting catcher this year. I mean, I can, but only because he took my position. But really, Kevin's probably the best catcher in the league now.

Since no one's figured out a way for Kevin to pitch and catch at the same time, I manage to get a couple of innings a week behind the plate.

It's hard to get a rhythm when I catch Kevin. He's a quick-pitcher. He relies too heavily on his fastball which, when he mixes it in with other pitches, is overpowering. But when it's all he throws, batters find a way to catch up with it.

You'd be surprised how easy it is to hit a fastball, if you know it's coming. I mean, it takes a while to awaken the reflexes so that you can react quickly enough to put that bat on a ball thrown pretty hard. It took me about two seasons. But now, when a pitcher has only one pitch and that pitch is smoke, I'm delighted. As is most of the league.

When I tell people I play in the over-30 hardball league, I can almost guarantee their response. Nearly everyone asks right away, "how fast do they throw in that league?" God! How rude. It's like admiring your pants, then asking your waist size. "Plenty hard," is what I usually tell them. They're basically asking how good you could possibly be, as if hitting an 80-mile-an-hour fastball is the only gauge of one's baseball talent. No one ever asks, "hey, do they hit cutoff men in that league?" or "how far apart are the bases in that league?"

After getting tossed from the Cardinal Gibbons High School baseball team, I was all but tossed from Cardinal Gibbons High School. "You can't expel me! I quit!" Everyone agreed it was best if I pursued my academic dreams within the Wake County public schools.

And while I wasn't exactly dean's list, nor was I the academic disaster I'd been at Gibbons. The Catholic high school was great for a lot of kids; a hothouse atmosphere where every move was scrutinized and analyzed.

Athens Drive High School was seven or eight times as large as Gibbons. No uniforms, no nuns, no weird morality classes.

Athens felt like a normal high school. Black kids, white kids, rich kids, poor kids. Kids who wanted to learn and kids who wanted to goof off.

I had an awful baseball tryout at Athens and, as a result, was relegated to the junior varsity. I was the oldest player on the JV team and paid very little attention that season. I can hardly remember a thing about it.

Seven

At four wins and no losses, the A's are having a ball. Well, nearly all of them are. The one Athletic who is not having any fun is Jack Richmond.

Jack joined the team in the middle of last season and, truthfully, he's awful. He's supposed to be a pitcher, but he can't throw strikes and he can't get anyone out. At the plate, he's the owner of the most pathetic swing in the league. Jack is totally flat-footed when he bats. He swings the bat using only his arms. No weight shift, no step toward the pitcher. It's like his shoes are nailed to the batter's box.

Hitting is just an inconvenience for Jack Richmond. What he really wants to do is pitch. He's gotten into a few games since he joined the A's and it's been pretty ugly each time. Here's how it goes: He walks a bunch of guys. He hits a few more guys. Somebody hits a rocket off him. DD comes to the mound, takes the ball from him and Jack gets mad at DD, believing the manager has a double standard. He'll leave Rod, Scott or any of the other pitchers in the game while they're taking a beating, but DD yanks Jack at the first sign of trouble.

Jack's half right. DD does have a quicker hook with him than with any of the other pitchers. But don't pitchers have to earn a manager's trust? Don't managers have to believe — even a little bit — that the pitcher is capable of finding his way out of a mess? When Jack gets into trouble, it's impossible to imagine him fighting his way through it. He huffs and puffs and bitches at the umpire. When the catcher throws the ball back to him, he swats at it belligerently with his glove. That's why DD won't leave him in. When Jack struggles, he's like a desperate poker player on a losing streak, betting everything in hopes of covering his losses. Bad idea.

95

The other reason Jack is unhappy is that he's isolated. He's never really tried to connect with the A's and they've made few attempts to connect with him. He shows up for games, warms up silently, plays and goes home. He's a bummer, really.

Today, we shut out the Hornets 8–0 for our fifth straight win. I didn't think we could get better than the last game, but we did. I handled five or six chances at third with no trouble at all. I played shallow at third base for almost every Hornets batter, defying them to hit one past me.

When I started the season at third, I was playing the position like a catcher. I knocked everything down with my chest and kept balls in front of me. Behind the plate, that's pretty much enough. At third, you have to actually catch balls cleanly to have any chance at throwing out runners. Since it's such a long throw from third base, even the slightest bobble can cost you the out. In only five games, I've gotten a lot more sure-handed at third. I have quick hands to make up for my not-so-quick feet.

I'm even starting to enjoy the position. Before every pitch, I crouch low and touch the ground in front of me with the back of my glove, reminding myself to stay down on ground balls. Against the Hornets, I threw out the fastest guy in the league trying to bunt for a hit. Manny Magaña dropped a surprise bunt in my direction and tore out of the box like a rabbit. I was already playing in, not anticipating a bunt, but knowing that to have any chance at all of throwing Manny out, I'd have to play way up on the grass part of the infield. At the last possible instant, Manny squared around and put down a textbook bunt. I charged the bouncing ball, caught it with my bare hand and, in the same motion, sidearmed the ball hard to Alex, stretched out at first base. It was close, but I got him.

The best part about making a play like that is watching the base umpire. Good base umpires will give the call a little soul on a close play. When the ball beat Manny by the tiniest margin, the umpire hopped quickly toward first, pointing down at the bag. "He got 'im!" the ump barked. He punched at the air in front of him. "Oooouuuuut!"

The play happened in front of the A's bench and the team, along with the handful of wives and girlfriends who came to the game, went bananas.

I collected two more hits against the Hornets. I was now officially hot. Death to the slump! Long live the hot streak! Vive le streak!

After the game, a bunch of us went to the bar, where Joe spent money like he hit the lottery.

Beer after beer in a dark bar on a Sunday summer afternoon. Sweaty, filthy and smelly, dressed like total goofs, the A's bonded. More beer. Some kind of unholy booze and shellfish alliance called an oyster shooter. Cigarettes. Lots of cigarettes. Dancing, hollering. More oyster shooters. I love the A's and the A's love me.

Right before my senior year of high school, my family picked up and moved to Maryland. My father heard the siren song of the big city and we headed north.

My mother and my sister weren't crazy about the idea. We'd been in Raleigh for 13 or 14 years. I loved the idea. My dad kept saying, "Baltimore's a really nice city." We'd visited Baltimore sort of by accident a few months earlier and I loved it. It seemed just right. Smaller than New York, but bigger and more sophisticated than Raleigh. More baseball and more punk rock.

But we didn't move to Baltimore. We moved to a town called Columbia, fifteen or twenty miles south of Baltimore.

It was like living in an After-School Special. Columbia, Maryland is one of those planned suburban communities where you can't see anyone's garbage cans and the gas stations are all underground. The main gathering place in Columbia is a gigantic shopping mall. The Gap and Macy's are Columbia's idea of community. My mother and my sister took a while to adjust, but they did adjust. I hated Columbia the moment we moved there and continued to hate it.

There was lots to dislike about Columbia, but the worst part was the street names. Some genius town planner thought it was a good idea to name Columbia's streets after snippets from poems. And not, like, Walt Whitman poems, either. Dippy poems that no one knew that featured lines about fairies and dew. It was awful. We lived on Corn

Tassel Court. You should just skip the middle part and name it "Please Kill Me Road" or "Kick My Ass Avenue."

In addition to a new town, it was time for a new start at another high school. I'd finally had some success in the 11th grade and now had to adjust to a new school.

Again, my sister blended right in. She made friends, she joined some clubs — all the stuff you're supposed to do at a new school.

I sleepwalked through most of my senior year of high school, making a few friends but mainly going to ballgames and punk shows by myself. My dad and I continued our weeknight tradition of going to ballgames, only now we went to Baltimore's Memorial Stadium instead of tiny little Durham Athletic Park.

I didn't bother going out for my high school baseball team at my new school. My grades were still recovering from my first two years of high school and, if I didn't want to wind up in the Marines or something, I was going to have to scramble to find a college that would take me.

Despite a solid C minus average, I got into college, where I would flail as aimlessly and teeter as precariously as I did in high school.

The summer before I started college, I played in a Columbia recreational league. When you move from one town to another, it takes years before you feel like you're no longer the new guy. Thus, despite having lived in Maryland for nearly a year, I didn't know anything about what leagues to join or what teams to pursue. I wound up a catcher on the sorriest team in the league, a team so awful it should never have been assembled.

Early in the season, we lost about nine straight and it became clear that the players all hated each other. Long, hot, demoralizing innings piled on top of one another. Our pitchers walked batter after batter, interrupted only by searing line drives. Our team committed errors in the field, errors on the bases, errors wherever they could be committed. Our infielders heckled their own pitchers. The outfielders could scarcely be bothered to chase down extra base hits. And as the catcher, I saw it all. Every run that scored stomped on home plate right in front of me.

In July of that year, after 19 or 20 games, I made my finest play of the season. I broke my left thumb.

Or rather, somebody else did. On a tapper back to the pitcher, a right-handed hitter swung his bat all the way around, corkscrewing himself into the soft batter's box. His enormous backswing hit the back of my catcher's mitt like a big, heavy hammer. It felt like someone dropped a piano on my thumb. I flung off my catcher's mitt and began leaping in the air bent over at the waist, like a baboon. I tucked my left hand tucked under my right arm and swore at top volume.

After the leaping stage came the writhing stage. Still protecting my crushed thumb, I rolled around in the dust behind home plate, still swearing. My dad was at the game and came out of the stands during my thumb hysterics. He bent over me while I wriggled in the dust. "Cut it out," he whispered, a little embarrassed by my display. "It's not that bad."

I was in agony and wasn't about to be denied my due. My dad helped me off the field and the umpire picked up my mitt and catcher's mask and flung them into our dugout, the mask rattling around under the bench. My thumb was now, just moments after getting whacked, swelling and a vivid purple. The nail was bright red, like I'd painted it.

I sat on the bench next to a cooler for a second, holding my left arm with my right. Dad was careful not to touch my thumb, but wanted to get a look at how bad it was.

"Here, lemme see," he said, reaching for my hand.

"Dad, no. C'mon," I pulled away. "Just a second."

"It's OK, lemme see."

I let go of my left hand. My dad took me by the wrist and plunged my arm into the cooler, full of ice and water. I yanked it back and all over again, like a cartoon, I swore and leapt around. My dad drove me the hospital.

About half way there, he said perhaps the only thing that could've, at that moment, distracted me from the pain: "Well, at least you won't have to play on that terrible team anymore."

It was true. I was relieved to be out for the remainder of the miserable season. But I hadn't realized that a broken thumb would be the end of baseball for me for another 15 years.

Eight

It's easy to let baseball consume me. I can easily float through six months of life thinking of nothing but the baseball season. I try not to do it anymore, but sometimes it's an effort.

In college, I made no such effort. A few weeks after I transferred to a school in Baltimore, I got a job on the Orioles grounds crew. It was so much easier than I imagined it would be. I was shocked to learn there wasn't a waiting list a mile long for a chance to run around on the field at Memorial Stadium and make $3.35 an hour at the same time.

But there was no line. Just a regular job interview with the assistant groundskeeper, a sullen Midwesterner named Dale Schultz. Dale had a cop's mustache and worked hard to mask his thinning hair. He'd earned some kind of advanced degree in groundskeeping and was considered one of the young stars in the field. So to speak.

Schultz sized me up and could tell I was enthusiastic about working for a big league team. He could tell because I mentioned a dozen times how enthusiastic I was to work for a big league team. I was hired on the spot.

The Orioles were a team in decline. Only a few faces remained from their glory years and the team was coming off a third straight disappointing season.

Following their 1983 World Series win over Philadelphia, the Orioles got a little worse every year. Instead of names like Al Bumbry and Ken Singleton, fans tried to warm up to Jim "The Whammer" Traber and Sugar Bear Rayford. Charming? Yeah. Talented? Not so much.

By 1988, even the charm was gone. Cal Ripken, Eddie Murray and Mike Boddicker were among the last World Series guys left. Boddicker was dealt to Boston late that summer. Murray hated Baltimore by then and pined publicly to be traded to his hometown Dodgers. Ripken's father was the manager, until he was fired after six games.

Fans will recall that team's historic futility. The Birds were swept in the first series of the season. Then the next. And the one after that. Cal's brother Bill Ripken got his picture on the cover of Sports Illustrated, seated on the O's bench, bent over, his forehead leaning on the knob of his bat. The headline read "0–18." And it would, of course, get even worse than that.

The Baltimore Orioles began the 1988 season with 21 straight losses, the gold standard for season-opening badness. They lost close ones. They lost blowouts. They lost to good teams and they lost to bad teams. By the time they finally beat the White Sox at Comiskey Park on April 29, the whole country knew about the Orioles' troubles.

I never cared. I was in the majors.

A day or two before that infamous season started, I got a call to get to the stadium as fast as I could. Plump black clouds taunted the city. The precious infield dirt was at risk. I imagined every grounds crew member across the city, looking worriedly at the sky all day, rubbing his chin, afraid to stray far from the telephone. I thought we should have some kind of device, like the Bat Signal, to let the grounds crew know it was time for them to drop whatever they were doing and get to the stadium.

When the call came, I reacted like a fireman. I jumped in my Volkswagen and laid a smoking patch of rubber on the street. Tires screeching, weaving in and out of traffic, I was sure the police would understand if they pulled me over for speeding and reckless driving. "Officer, let me go! I'm on the grounds crew!"

I made it to the stadium in minutes. Since there was no game, the parking lot was empty. Bouncing all over the potholed parking lot, I zoomed straight up next to Gate W4 and yanked the parking brake in the spot marked "Groundskeeper." I got out of my car and entered the dark hole in the side of the stadium on a full sprint, exploding through the grounds crew clubhouse door. Inside, nine or ten high school kids were sleeping or watching TV.

"Where the fuck have you been?" my new boss rapid-fired.

"I got here as fast as I could," I said, out of breath. "Is the field OK?"

"What do you mean is the field OK? What the fuck business is it of yours?"

"Uh... none. I just thought..."

"Yeah? Well don't. You're not here to think."

Given Schultz's disapproval of my arrival time, I figured the crew would be unrolling the tarp at any minute. But we didn't. We just sat around, waiting. I had no idea what we were waiting for but I wasn't about to ask the Tarp Nazi. He didn't need a reason to ask where the fuck you'd been. He just asked it. Apparently, once you crossed the line into the deep recesses of a baseball stadium, all rules of civility were lifted. Inside the ballpark, people lived by a different code.

Turns out, those snoozing high school kids were on the grounds crew too. They lived in the neighborhood. It took them about forty seconds to get to the park.

I walked out of the clubhouse to the dormant baseball diamond. The huge stadium was completely empty and silent. As a grounds crew guy, I was fully authorized to walk on the field, but had to defy my instinct to stay put and be content to lean over the rail. Countless times, I'd been to ballgames, but never walked on a big league field. I entered through a little gate in the wall and stood on the grey shale warning track, looking down at the foul line. Wood. The foul line was made of a long two-by-four laid into the ground. Huh. I'll be damned.

I walked softly across the line and stood in the impossibly soft outfield grass, trying to memorize the panorama. The horseshoe-shaped stadium wrapped around me. It's an unusual perspective; when you're a fan at a game, you face the field. When you're on the field, you face the fans. And when there are no fans, you face an ocean of colorful empty chairs.

I stopped in center field and closed my eyes. I imagined all the centerfielders who stood where I was standing. I could feel their presence all around me. Al Bumbry and Garry Maddox in the 1983 World Series. Omar Moreno in the 1979 Series. Mickey Mantle in the 50s and 60s.

I was submerged in baseball history when the rest of the grounds

103

crew stampeded onto the field, sprinting past third base toward the tarp, rolled up against the first base rail. I opened my eyes and took off from center field and joined the charging herd, wondering why suddenly everyone was in such a hurry. In seconds, the giant filthy tarp was swarming with grounds crew guys, pushing the beast toward first base.

"Let's go! Let's go! Move your asses," Schultz shouted, the first raindrops falling gently. He may have been a Tarp Nazi, but he could predict a rainstorm to the minute.

I took a position on the tarp line and pushed with everything I had. The white tarp was caked with red dirt and stunk like sour milk. It rolled recalcitrantly toward a spot behind first base. When we got to the foul line, Tarp Nazi instructed us to step on the loose flap of the tarp so that it could begin unrolling.

Immediately, the thing felt a million pounds lighter. The beast seemed to unravel on its own now, spraying up an unholy mold culture that had colonized since the last time the tarp encountered the light of day.

One by one, as the tarp made a thick white stripe in shallow right field, crew members dropped off the line and took positions at its edge from right field to center field. Raining steadier now, it felt good to be working so hard on a big league baseball field. Running, sweating, getting dirty — it was a little like being a big leaguer.

I grabbed my piece of the tarp, near second base, peeking over my shoulder toward home plate, knowing this was the view major league infielders got.

Again, I was startled from a baseball trance.

"Who the fuck took my fucking parking space? Goddammit, which one of you shitheads took my parking space?" Echoing vulgarities bounced around the empty canyon of a stadium.

The vitriol spewed from a familiar face. It was Pat Santarone, beloved Baltimore groundskeeper. He was a local celebrity. Everybody knew him. His smiling mug was on commercials for supermarkets and lawncare products. He did a regular segment on the news, giving people tips on keeping their grass as green as the Orioles kept theirs. The chubby, popular Miracle-Gro pitchman was stomping red-faced in my direction, under a huge orange umbrella. The only thing I could think was that Santarone's wild fury was an odd match for his avuncular persona. It was like getting charged by Howdy Doody.

"Is that your piece of shit car?" he screamed in my face. "Hey! I'm talking to you, goddammit!"

"Wh... which one?"

The tarp lay limp on the grass, waiting for the grounds crew to wrangle it again. The crew, meanwhile stood expressionless in the rain and watched Santarone berate me. Just when you thought his rage was at its peak, Santarone found a new level.

"WHAT THE FUCK DO YOU MEAN, WHICH ONE?" The hate in his eyes was alarming. Veins in his big, red head quivered as he screamed. "THE ONE PARKED IN THE FUCKING SPOT THAT SAYS 'GROUNDSKEEPER!' THAT ONE, YOU FUCKING TURD!"

"Oh yeah. That's mine."

"Well you better goddam well move it before I have it towed and blowed up! You stupid shit!"

"Sure! Yeah! Sorry!"

He mocked me. "Sooorrry. I'm soooorrry. Oooh I'm so soooory." He looked like an idiot, prancing around under his umbrella, making fun of me. When he got tired of it, he asked me, "Where'd you say you go to school?"

"Towson State, Mr. Santarone."

"Don't they teach you to fucking read there? The sign says 'Groundskeeper parking only,' shit-for-brains."

I thought I *was* a groundskeeper.

A cold drizzle — not to mention the Milwaukee Brewers — took a lot of the fun out of Opening Day for Orioles fans. After dropping the season-opening two-game series at home to the Brewers, the O's lost three in Cleveland. They returned home to more cold rain and the Kansas City Royals.

But I don't think I even noticed the lousy weather until someone pointed out that my boxer shorts were clearly visible through my rain soaked white pants. Not just any boxer shorts, either. My red, gold and white Maryland Terrapins boxer shorts. As my pants got wetter and wetter from the rain, big smiling snapping turtles became clearly visible through my cheap uniform pants.

The uniforms made the grounds crew look like 20 Good Humor men, running all around. Super-starched, tight, white pants, a scratchy white shirt with "Orioles" in block letters on the back. Inexplicably, we all had numbers on the left front pocket of our uniform shirts. I took great pride that my number was 33, same as Orioles first baseman Eddie Murray.

Before the game, my job was to help disassemble the batting cage and roll it away from home plate. Five minutes before knockdown time, I made my way to home plate alongside a handful of colleagues. The other Crew guys couldn't have cared less. They were checking out girls in the crowd, punching each other in the arm and generally acting like high school goofballs.

But I couldn't believe what I was seeing. I was watching major league batting practice up close. The visiting Royals were taking batting practice only a few feet in front of me. Then I spotted him.

Ask me who my all-time favorite player is and I'll laugh at you. It's like your favorite song or your favorite book or movie. It depends on my mood. Sometimes it's Eddie Murray. Sometimes it's Cal Ripken. Or Manny Sanguillen. Or Willie Stargell. But at least half the time, my favorite player is George Brett.

I always admired Brett, though I never cared one way or another for his team. During the years when Kansas City and the Yankees met in the playoffs, George Brett's ferocity caught my eye. A lot of young players find a big leaguer they emulate. George Brett was my guy. When I played for Alan the Foulmouthed Dwarf, he put me at third base and told me to watch the Royals as often as I could. Watch the third baseman. That's how you play ball. Like him.

I took Alan's advice and became a disciple. I batted left-handed, wore number five, chewed tobacco. All of it.

Now, here he was, right in front of me, whacking pitch after pitch all over Memorial Stadium. I had to tell him what a fan I was. I mean, he'd want to know, right?

Brett came out of the batting cage and stood next to me, leaning on the metal bar. Aw shit. How do you strike up a conversation with your hero without becoming a total dork? "Hey, Mr. Brett!" No. Not that. How about "Nice hitting, Mr. Brett!"? What's with the Mr. Brett thing? Call him George! He's a public figure. He's used to it. But for the love of God, call him something. He's gonna walk away any second now!

"Fnungh," is what I said as I turned and extended a hand for Mr. Brett to shake. I was so nervous I couldn't get a word out of my mouth. Only a syllable. And not a very good one, either. And just as I uttered that little piece of wisdom, George Brett made a break for a few last swings in the cage before batting practice was over. Only there was something lodged between him and home plate: me.

You know those awkward moments when, no matter how hard you try, you can't get out of a person's way? Move this way. Ha! You moved that way too! No, wait. Now this way! Hey! You went that way too! Silly! That's how it goes. It's a wacky misunderstanding. Except, when you get into one of those things with George Brett, he gets all pissed off, yells "Get out of my way, dickhead!" and grabs you by the back of your shirt collar and throws you into the batting net, which doesn't much cushion your fall or keep your feet from flying up in the air, really showing off those smiling turtle undershorts to the crowd.

Nine

Nothing like a rainout to kill a team's momentum.

We got rained out against the Chargers and had a whole week to try to stay hot. One night during the week, I went to a batting cage out in the suburbs to keep my swing going. I'm of the opinion that hitting off a machine when you're on a hot streak doesn't do you any good. And probably does you more than a little harm. Hitting has everything to do with timing. It's a little like dancing with the pitcher, sixty feet, six inches apart. Your moves in the batter's box are in direct response to his moves on the mound. The batter rocks back and forth a little, trying to find a groove. The pitcher uses his body to get something behind his pitches. You're moving together, the pitcher leading. Is that weird?

But hitting off a machine is like dancing with a machine. There's no timing at all, no soul, nothing for the hitter to respond to. The ball just comes blazing out of a hole in a fence, slung from between two spinning rubber tires. I guess it could be good for reflexes or hand-eye coordination. But it's impossible to find any rhythm when you're not responding to an actual pitcher. I might get a bat on the first five or six balls that come in, maybe even hit one or two of them hard. But then, anticipating a rhythm, I'm swinging way ahead of the next six or seven balls. All my considerable weight is on my front foot, producing only foul balls and little tappers back toward the cursed contraption. And by the time the last couple balls come in, I'm winded and have no timing at all. When you're trying to preserve a hot streak, hitting off a pitching machine is the wrong thing to do.

Which didn't stop me from doing it. I never remember how bad those things mess up my swing until I've sunk $20 worth of tokens into them. I flailed at pitch after pitch and left sweaty and clueless. I even tried to hit right-handed, just to make sure my timing was completely ruined.

There's no explaining why I throw right-handed but bat left-handed. Really, there just isn't. There must be some explanation why it feels utterly foreign and unnatural for me to stand in the third base batter's box. I've tried all kinds of techniques to learn to switch hit. I can't do it.

For one, my hands feel weird. I never think of how natural my baseball swing is until I try to do it right-handed. It's all out of rhythm. It feels like a lot of little pieces that don't fit together. The feet, the hands, the eye. That's the worst part — the eye. It's like I'm trying to see the ball with my right eye, rather than my left, which is closer to the pitcher. It's just all wrong.

Actually, I feel like I do bat right-handed, since my right eye dominates when I hit. And my swing is powered by my right arm. When I swing, it's like a tennis backhand. I drag the bat through the hitting zone with my right arm. The left arm adds a little power, but mainly it's for guidance.

I have classic lefthander's swing. I take great pride in an easy, level swing. Even when I'm in a slump, lost at the plate, my swing looks good. That should count for something, I think.

When I turn over my top hand — my left hand — my hips are open and my weight is shifting from the back foot to the front. Since I have short arms, my swing is compact. As soon as the bat is through the zone, my top hand comes off and I begin the follow through that is unique to lefthanders. The swing finishes with the bat in my right hand, my head down, my right arm extended high in the air. Think yoga.

I think somehow my partial left-handedness has kept me from being much of a power hitter. I'd like nothing more than to hit a couple home runs a year. And I'm a strong guy, built with some heft that should translate into some pop.

But I'm not. I'm good for some gappers, but mainly I'm a singles hitter. When I'm on, I can hit for a decent average. When I get my favorite pitch to hit — fastball down and in — and I wrap around it, I immediately think I've cranked one out of the park. And it's fair by plenty until, inevitably, it hooks dramatically and lands harmlessly in the grass, a few feet right of the foul line. There's just something in the physics of my swing that prevents a home run from staying fair. The only way I can generate enough power to go deep is to hit the ball so deep into my swing that the English on the ball propels it foul. Every time it happens, our bench chatters about straightening it out. They want to see a homer. God knows, I want to hit one. And that's the worst thing you can think. Because I don't think I've ever gotten a hit after one of those long foul balls. I'm feeling like Babe Ruth and the pitcher knows it. He throws me a pitch I hate — up and away, slow — that I try to turn on. Dink. Out.

Like nearly all left-handed hitters I hate hitting off left-handed pitchers. But here's the weird part — I usually hit them pretty well.

I don't hit them hard, but pretty often I can punch a hit off them.

Hitting off a lefthander feels all wrong. It makes me claustrophobic. It's like being crowded into a corner. The ball comes from behind you and bears down on you. It's so uncomfortable that my aim is just to put the ball in play. If there's a runner on base, I try to move him up. But my swing is so defensive that, pretty often, I'm able to muscle a hit through the infield, which plays me to pull no matter who's pitching.

By the time our game against the Over-30 Giants finally rolled around, I had a bad feeling. The Giants won the league championship last year and the year before that. They've played together for years, they hit like monsters and their pitchers are smart. They're easily the best team in the league.

This week's game is a clash of the titans. We're 5–0 and the Giants are 5–1, having dropped an extra innings game to the Vikings the day before we were rained out last week.

Tim Gaudet walked the first Giant of the game. And the second. Their third batter, Nick Fowlkes hit a double back up the middle that nearly undressed Tim, like when Charlie Brown gets his clothes knocked off by a line drive. It's not easy to hit a double up the middle. The ball shot past the pitcher and zoomed over the centerfielder's head like the Blue Angels doing a flyover. The Giants' barrage continued until we finally got the third out after the fifth run scored. A five-run first inning put something of a damper on the game, especially after the rainout. We sleepwalked through the game and lost 12–6.

The Giants, more than any other team in the league, actually pay attention to their games. They keep scouting reports on every hitter in the league. Which is why I didn't get a hit today. Their infield puts a Ted Williams-style lefthander shift on when I come up, defying me to try to hit the ball to the third base side. I'm flattered, really, that anyone's paid that much attention to my hitting style. When I'm in the batter's box and I see the shortstop playing where the second baseman should be, the only thing I can think is, "Aw, you shouldn't have. For me?" While I guess I am a pull hitter, it's not like I don't go the other way once in a while. But the shift's effect on me is purely psychological. It's like when you're playing basketball and you find yourself completely unguarded, wide open. That's the toughest shot to hit.

With the shift on, I get a pitch I think I can crush and hit a bloop behind first base. Hey, it's better than nothing, I tell myself. A hit's a hit. But this isn't a hit at all. The second baseman is playing behind first base, practically on the foul line. He moves two steps to his right and makes the catch. Which is pretty much how the whole game went.

Our first loss knocked us out of first place. Jeez, this is a tough league.

One of the jobs that most grounds crew guys hated was bullpen duty. It meant that you spent the whole game in the bullpen, ready to cover the pitching mounds in case it rained. Or open and close the gate for when a relief pitcher was brought in. That was it.

I loved working in the bullpen. It meant I got to sit in the little open faced wooden shed and watch the game with the pitchers. It was fascinating to watch a baseball game with big league players and coaches.

Inexplicably, bullpen duty was a two-man affair. Schultz assigned two guys to the Orioles bullpen every night and two more to the visitors pen.

The cardinal rule on bullpen duty was this: do not bug the pitchers. Don't talk to them. Don't pester them. Don't ask them for anything. And, if you're in the visitors bullpen, do not, under any circumstances, let them know you're rooting for the Orioles.

It's obvious that the Orioles grounds crew would root for the Orioles. But it was bad form to show it in front of the other team. If something made the home crowd cheer, the grounds crew guy in the visitors bullpen had to be quiet.

The Mariners were in town and I was assigned to their bullpen with Johnny Morton, a nerdy high school kid who appeared physically unable to stop talking. Johnny was a nervous talker, a play-by-play announcer of life. He described everything he saw, compulsively and in annoying detail. "Hey, nice shoes. Where's you get those shoes? Foot Locker, huh? Yeah, there's a Foot Locker down the block from me. Nice stuff. Real nice. I don't go in much. Kinda pricey. My mom takes me to Shoe City, downtown. You know where that is? Yeah, yeah. That's the one." He would sing the commercial. "Your ci-ty, my ci-ty, I said Shoe Ci-taaaaaay." Johnny was endearing—completely harmless—but had to the capacity to jangle the nerves of even the calmest people. Schultz used to give him bullpen duty just so he didn't have to be anywhere near him.

The kid was OK in the Orioles bullpen. Elrod Hendricks, the late, longtime Baltimore coach who ruled the O's bullpen for years, liked Johnny and didn't mind his non-stop chatter. Johnny's jitters made him laugh. But Johnny was dangerous in the visitors bullpen.

The Orioles and M's played a tense, close late-season game. Johnny, unable to cope with the tension in the little bullpen shed, chattered at twice his usual pace.

"Batterstepsout. Kicksalittledirtaround. Looksatthe third-basecoachforthesign. Stepsbackinandwavesthebataround. Pitchernodsatthecatcherandwindsup. Thepitch. Groundball. Groundballtoshort. Calgrabsitandthrowstofirstfortheout."

"Jeezus, kid! Will you knock it off?" pleaded the Seattle bullpen coach after too many innings of play by play. "You're killin' me."

"Sorrysorrysorry." Johnny said.

"He can't really help it, sir," I said to the Seattle coach, who wasn't looking at me. "He can't stop talking."

113

"Can't stop," Johnny said. "Can'tstoptalking. Talkingallthetime."

The bullpen coach rolled his eyes and tried to concentrate on the game.

I told Johnny to stand outside the little bullpen house, away from the Seattle players. He did and peace was restored as Johnny kept his running commentary confined to the empty chairs next to the pitchers mounds.

But as the Orioles continued their rally, the phone rang in the Mariners bullpen and two pitchers supplanted Johnny in the warmup area. He returned to the little house, sitting on a bench in the corner, next to a bucket of candy the Seattle pitchers had brought from the clubhouse. I looked at Johnny and made a "shh" sign with a finger over my lips. He nodded furiously, wincing like he was going to burst. It took every ounce of energy he had to remain quiet.

One of the bullpen pitchers was called into the game. And I took a seat next to Johnny, to try to keep him quiet.

The coach sat with his elbows on his knees at the other end of the shed, nervously chewing his fingernails and spitting.

With a runner at second late in a tie game, the relief pitcher fell behind in the count to Orioles favorite Eddie Murray. The pitcher grooved one down the middle and Murray connected. Johnny made a squeak and grabbed my knee as the ball climbed higher and higher into the night, headed our way. Seattle centerfielder Henry Cotto raced back to the wall and looked up as the ball the cleared the fence by an inch, bouncing on the cement inside the shed and ricocheting around like a bullet.

Johnny screamed and threw his hands above his head "Yaaaaaaa-hahahaha! Whooooohoooo!" He jumped up and knocked over the bucket of candy, sending Clark bars and Bit o Honeys bouncing around the shed. "Yeahbaby! It'sgone! Homerun, EddieMurray!"

The Seattle bullpen coach lost his mind.

"Get out! Goddammit get him the fuck out of my sight!" He was swatting his sky blue Mariner cap at Johnny and me, moving toward us like he might kill us. "You can't fucking root for the other team in here! Get out! Now! I mean it! Don't ever let me see you assholes in here again!"

I grabbed Johnny by the shirt and pulled him out of the shed. He was repeating every word the coach said and holding the home run ball over his head, leaping up and down, waving to the cheering crowd in the bleachers.

Memorial Stadium had its own economy; its own cultures and subcultures. In addition to the official ballpark economy that the fans were subject to, the ballpark workers had their own elaborate market, built on supply and demand.

Vendors, grounds-crew guys, clean-up crews, ushers and ticket window people traded commodities all season.

The walk-around vendors didn't participate much in the stadium's meta-economy. Their dealings were actual cash transactions: they bought beer or hot dogs or pretzels at wholesale price from some ballpark supplier, then walked around and sold it to the fans. Once in a while, late in a sparsely attended game, a pretzel or hot dog guy would come to the grounds crew pit and offer cheap food, just so he didn't get completely stuck with a batch of perishable food.

The beer guys didn't have that problem. Cans of beer could wait until tomorrow or the next homestand to pay dividends. Beer guys were pros who didn't need the underground ballpark economy. You'd see a lot of them working the aisles at other sporting events in the area. The Memorial Stadium beer guys all worked at the Preakness, hawking watered down booze to throngs of gambling drunks. You'd see them selling programs at Maryland football games or cheap party crap downtown on New Year's Eve. They were salesmen.

An urban myth floated around the stadium and around the city that Baltimore's best beer vendors were, if not exactly wealthy, then at least very well off. They were rumored to live in expensive neighborhoods. Budweiser and other giant breweries were said to fly the Orioles' beer vendors to the Super Bowl and the World Series every year to hustle hops with their distinctive sales pitches.

Everybody knew the beer guys: Fancy Clancy. Robo-Can. Peanuts. The Sergeant. Like the Orioles themselves, they hung high above the rest of the stadium riff raff.

But while the Orioles and the beer guys enjoyed the top of the stadium caste system, even the visiting teams participated in Memorial Stadium's underground markets.

Grounds crew duty in the visitors bullpen meant potential quid pro quo favors for the out of town pitchers. During the first game of the series, pitchers would ask college age grounds crew guys where to pick up girls in Baltimore. If the pitchers had a particularly successful postgame experience, they sometimes would give the grounds crew tipster a hat or a jacket from the visiting team. I once got a Tigers sweatshirt after steering a Detroit reliever to Max's on Broadway in Fells Point.

From time to time, reliever requests were more exotic than information on Baltimore nightlife.

With his team riding a hot streak, a veteran American League closer called me over before the game's first pitch. I was minding the visitors bullpen and the closer told me he had a deal for me. After furtive looks to the left and right to make sure the coast was clear, he unzipped a leather equipment bag with his team's logo on it and revealed six bottles of Michelob, swaddled lovingly in a couple of towels to keep the glass bottles from clinking together. The pitcher had earned a save in each of the past three games and was told by his manager that he had the night off to rest his arm.

Of course, that didn't mean he was free to drink six beers in the bullpen. That's where he needed my help. If I distracted his bullpen coach while he poured the beer from the bottles into a plastic cup, the closer said he'd give me his hat at the end of the game and a big bag of baseballs at the end of the series. Fair enough, I thought.

I stashed the pitcher's beer bag behind the bullpen house. Every couple innings, the closer took a casual stroll around to the back of the bullpen house while I put on a show for the bullpen coach. I started stretching in front of him, doing it all wrong so he'd tell me the right way to do it. I raked the pitchers mounds. I cleaned the shed. Whatever it took to get his attention. We went through the routine enough times for the six-pack to be history. The coach had no idea.

I gave the closer credit; he could really hold his beer. He didn't act like a drunk at a ballgame. He had a happy glow after six beers in a couple hours. And he clapped and danced a little to the music on the stadium public address system between innings. But that could've been attributed to his team's hot streak. He kept an even temper and didn't do anything stupid.

In the game's late innings, 10 or 15 minutes after the last beer was gone, the phone rang. The bullpen coach told a righthander and a left-hander to warm up. Knowing he had the night off, the closer watched the game happily from the bench in the bullpen house while the late-inning setup guys warmed up. Both pitchers eventually were called into the game. The visitors clung to a one run lead heading to the top of the ninth. After the eighth inning, the closer was grooving to whatever tunes the stadium public address system played. Stretching his legs, he stood in front of the bullpen house, looking past the scoreboard into the night, swaying and snapping his fingers. He was enjoying the game. Until the phone rang. The manager told the bullpen coach to get the closer ready. "But Skip told me I wasn't pitching tonight," the closer said, a little panicky. The bullpen coach grunted, "Yeah, well he changed his mind. Get ready."

The closer gave me a quick glance and removed his warmup jacket. He began throwing to the bullpen catcher, easy at first, then harder. It was nearly impossible to tell he'd just finished six beers. He did teeter just a little during one of his windups. But nobody noticed.

Sure enough, when his team failed to score in the top of the ninth, the phone rang and the closer was called upon to wrap up the game.

I opened up the gate in the outfield wall. "Here goes nothing," he said as he headed for the mound.

He pitched a one-two-three inning and earned the save. I never did get the baseballs and the hat, though.

Even when you play for the same team every year, your team's personality changes from season to season. My first few years on the team, the A's were paranoid and hostile. We had no chemistry, no sense of humor and no patience — for the game or for each other. Really, if I hadn't been so thrilled to be playing baseball again, I'd have left. The personality and the tone of my first three seasons varied a little, but basically, we were a sour, joyless group.

We're still sour and joyless, but I can't imagine playing for any other team. I belong to the A's. In a weird way, I'm proud to play for this team. We're a team that nobody can figure out. But neither do they want to play us.

My first three seasons with the A's, we finished with a losing record. We never had practice. Joe would scream and swear at us. Guys didn't show up on time, or call if they couldn't make it. Some days it was hard to field a team at all. More than once, I felt like I was playing for the Telephone Pioneers all over again. Except the A's uniforms weren't flannel.

People associated with the league identify players with their teams. It's natural. If you play for a team full of goons, you're perceived as a goon. If you play for a team with a reputation for choking, you're a choker. Every team in the league has a personality, made up of the strongest personalities on the team. If the loudest guy on your team is a lout, it won't be long before your team is seen as a bunch of louts. I like to think I'm not a lout. But around town, when I run into guys from other teams, I'm sure they say to their wives, "There's number nine for the A's. He's an asshole."

Well, I'm not an asshole. But I do play for the A's.

Ten

Just to make sure our hot streak was really snuffed out, the Baseball Gods rained out our next game. Now the team's rhythm is totally thrown off.

Most people think baseball and rain don't go together. That's probably true. The game itself and rain don't mix too well. But when you're on the grounds crew, rainy nights are when you really earn your $3.35 an hour.

If the game was already going on and rain started to fall, the whole grounds crew sat perched in our little pen down the left-field line. The tarp rested on the opposite end of the field, against the first-base box seat railing. Then, if harder rain was in the forecast, between innings the crew would jog to the other side of the field and crouch behind the tarp, ready to roll as soon as the umpire decided the rain was too hard.

Umpires usually waited as long as possible to call for rain delays. Thus, when the umpire crew chief finally threw his hands in the air to signal a delay, the field was already pretty soaked. The grounds crew had to work extra fast, unrolling the tarp from its metal tube to a spot in short right field. Then the crew had to scatter and line up at the giant tarp's edge, each man grabbing one of the handles sewn into the canvas. When Schultz gave the sign, we pulled as hard as we could, dragging the handle toward the third base line. The tarp hissed as it rubbed against itself. Once the sprinting grounds crew members got just past the pitcher's mound, the tarp fought back, snapping our shoulders and slamming our momentum to a halt. By then, the rain was usually pounding the field hard enough form little puddles in the baselines. As we dragged the beast the last few feet, our shoes skidded in the baseline mud. The precious infield at last covered, we drove metal tent stakes through the handles, to prevent the tarp from blowing away.

As the season progressed, I fell into a predictable grounds crew routine. I'd get to the park two and a half hours before game time. Change clothes at my locker. Watch a little TV in the clubhouse with the other grounds crew guys. I was the only college student on the grounds crew. The rest of the guys were either still in high school or worked during the day. Despite my terrible grades at school, on the grounds crew, I was known as the Genius.

For weekday games, by the time most of the grounds crew was getting dressed, the clubhouse television was tuned to the five-thirty broadcast of "Jeopardy." My crewmates gathered and marveled as I never missed an answer. I blurted out the most obscure literary and scientific references, one after another.

"Who is King Lear?"

"Whoa! Dude!"

"What is the Marshall Plan?"

"Again! The Genius!"

"Who was Stonewall Jackson?"

"Goddamm!"

What I never admitted, though, was that "Jeopardy" aired on another station at four o'clock. My roommates and I never missed it. After classes, we gathered in the house for our favorite quiz show. As soon as it was over, I'd go to the ballpark, the answers still fresh in my mind. Even Schultz and Santarone were impressed. The Genius lived.

After Jeopardy and in full uniform, I'd walk outside to the stadium's grounds crew area, down by the tomato plants that grew against the stands behind third base. The tomato plants were a tradition begun in the Orioles' glory years. Santarone and Hall of Fame manager Earl Weaver had contests to see which man could grow better tomatoes. They built a little planter box out of plywood and the plants grew up the side of the wall, toward the left field box seats. After Weaver retired, Santarone continued his tomato patch. It was a pretty charming tradition, if you didn't know better. Santarone's temper and miserable disposition made me root against his tomatoes. The whole grounds crew cheered when the Indians' Brook Jacoby hit a rocket foul ball that, after buzzing just over our heads, smoked about four tomato plants, splattering a few prize-winners all over the wall.

Chores finished, just before the game started, I ran up to the stadium concourse to grab some dinner.

I got friendly with a girl who worked at a stand near our clubhouse. We weren't supposed to get free food, but she was usually good for a hot dog and as many french fries as I could stuff into the plastic cup I brought up. I'd smother the dog and fries in ketchup and be in my favorite seat next to the field by first pitch.

Before each game, just like a lineup card, Schultz posted a list of ballpark chores with last names next to them. The assignments were things like batting practice breakdown, bullpen duty and — the biggest pressure cooker of them all — the fifth inning drag.

The drag was a physically demanding piece of choreography that, if performed perfectly, was a work of art. But one misstep could ruin the whole thing.

The goal was for the grounds crew to smooth the infield just before the top of the fifth inning. Five innings of major league baseball had mussed the precious dirt. We were to comb it and style it in preparation for the game's late innings. The drag was a five-man job: four draggers and a raker. The draggers pulled big metal mats with spikes and barbs from one end of the infield to the other, breaking up little dirt clods that might produce bad hops. The raker smoothed the spot just in front of first base where excess from the draggers' heavy mats left a little pile of dirt.

With one out in the bottom of the fourth, the draggers and the raker grabbed what they needed and lined up, single file. The instant the Orioles made the third out, we shot through the gate one after another with our mats under our arms. The draggers sprinted to third base from left field and, one at a time, unfurled our barbed mats so that they landed flat and smacked the dirt. Pulling the mats by their nylon ropes, we jogged around the infield while the mats dug their little barbs into the earth. We fanned out, so that our four mats covered the width of half of the infield, with virtually no overlap. We all made the turn at first base, now moving to the inner half of the infield. By now, the Orioles had taken the field and were warming up for the next inning. The first baseman rolled easy ground balls to the infielders, who scooped them up and fired them back. The O's had to maneuver their warmups around the grounds crew. It was just about as close to the players as we ever got. A few times dragging my mat past the shortstop position after Cal Ripken had homered in the bottom of the fourth, I said "nice shot, Cal." He winked and said thanks.

Pulling the heavy mat around by a thick, nylon rope was nearly impossible in wet weather. Red infield clay caked in the bottom instantly, gathering more wet dirt all along the way. By the end of the drag, I could hardly lift the mud-soaked thing. The sprint back to the grounds crew pit was grueling. For one thing, the mat weighed a ton. For another thing, my ill-fitting uniform pants inched lower and lower. Nothing looked worse than using one arm to lug the drag mat, while holding your pants up with the other. All, of course, while running as fast as you can back to the grounds crew pit, while the fans laughed their asses off. And if you were lucky, they'd put your fat ass up on the big stadium screen. It looked like one of those dumb games people play at office picnics.

While the roster of draggers rotated every night, the raker was always the same: the senior member of the Orioles grounds crew, Tom DiStefano.

A veteran of heaven know how many years on the crew, Tom was a divorced sports addict whose wardrobe included not one stitch of clothing that wasn't emblazoned with some kind of cheesy sports logo. Tom feathered his thinning hair and cultivated a flesh-colored mustache. By day, he worked at some kind of manufacturing plant in Baltimore's eastern industrial district.

But by night, Tom was the big honcho on the grounds crew, for what that was worth. Which wasn't much.

He carried himself like a pro wrestler, strutting around the grounds crew clubhouse, peppering unclever insults at anyone who ranked below him in the stadium caste system. His favorite — and only — witticism involved responding to anything anyone said to him by repeating the verb of the sentence and following it with "this" while grabbing his crotch. "Hey Tom, how 'bout grabbing that rake?"

"Hey, Pat, how 'bout grabbing this? Huh huh."

That part was important, too. The "huh huh."

"Nice Tom."

"Hey, nice this! Huh huh."

"Sure, Tom. That's plenty funny."

"Hey, plenty of this! Huh huh."

Tom's dimwitted assaults were fascinating. How was it possible to never tire of the same dumb gag? And the accompanying squeeze he gave his package seemed a little too pleasurable, like maybe Tom might like to be left alone for a few minutes.

On nights where the tarp wasn't needed, the innings that followed the drag were uneventful, as grounds crew duties went. And since the Orioles were often hopelessly behind by that point in the game, grounds crew members were usually forced to find their own entertainment. Some played cards in the clubhouse. Some watched TV. Some chatted with fans. A small group of us stuck together and watched every inning of every game, like it was some weird mission. Like flagpole sitting or a dance marathon.

In the late innings, during pitching changes or between innings, when the stadium PA system blasted pop songs to entertain fans, the four or five of us who stuck out every pitch regularly did some kind of silly dance to alleviate the boredom. Now, fans get on TV all time doing silly dances between innings. But when you have five guys in white uniforms, dancing and lip-synching to Gladys Knight and the Pips at a ballgame, you're sure to find them in the highlights. And we were. A couple times a week, home from the ballpark, drinking beer and watching ESPN, I regularly saw myself and my grounds crew colleagues doing a perfectly synchronized monkey or swim on SportsCenter. That's when you know you're in the big leagues.

Since it's still raining and there's nothing else to do, this is a good time to consider an important part of the game that we too often take for granted: the baseball handshake.

The baseball handshake has become an awkward affair. Sort of like those words in other languages that mean hello and goodbye at the same time, the baseball handshake serves a lot of purposes. It says, "Hey, way to go." Or it says, "Hey, get 'em next time." It's like buying a greeting card that says, "Thinking of you." It's a pretty cheap way to express whatever you're trying to express.

After big league games, the only players to shake hands are the winners. In every other sport, the two teams shake hands with one another, showing a spirit of sportsmanship and admiration. Not baseball. The catcher shakes hands with the pitcher, the infielders gather around, the dugout empties and the team celebrates its newborn victory. The losers skulk off.

But at every level of amateur baseball, opposing teams shake hands with each other. The postgame handshake has become a formality, an obligation to be gotten over with. When a game in our league is over, each team spontaneously forms a line. The two lines move past one another, giving each player a chance to shake hands with each player on the other team. But the players raise a right hand and walk through the line slapping hands, like they're running their hands along a picket fence. Why bother?

The umpires even encourage it. "C'mon, guys, shake 'em up!" Like your dad used to do when you got into a fight with a sibling. The handshake never meant anything; it was merely an indignity. Both parties knew that.

I'm a fan of the handshake. But it's become overwrought. For me, anyway. Too much can go wrong.

The difference between a baseball handshake and an everyday life handshake is this: you don't shake hands every day with everybody at your job, over and over again. In life, you shake hands when you meet someone or when you want to congratulate someone.

Baseball players can't stop shaking hands. We shake hands when someone succeeds. We shake hands when someone fails. We shake hands on the bench, for no other reason than we can't think of anything to say.

All of which is probably why ballplayers have come up with so many variations on the handshake theme.

Today, there are three basic baseball handshakes. There's the classic handshake that you use everywhere else in your life. The strong grip, the look in the eye. It's an earnest offering of a brief moment of your life.

There's the high five and each of its variations. Done properly, the high five can be a perfect exchange. It's easy to spot when someone offers a high five. You can respond quickly to it. And if both high fivers are about the same height, the high five can produce a satisfying slap, with a stinging aftertaste. In a lot of cases, a pair's momentum will propel each in opposite directions, allowing for a clean break. No long term commitments with the high five.

And then, there's the fist bump. I'm not sure who invented the fist bump, but I don't think I'd like him. I imagine he's trendy and has Pat Reilly hair.

The fist bump requires quick reflexes. It comes from nowhere. Suddenly, knuckles appear. With the fist bump, it's all or nothing. You either connect perfectly, each knuckle immediately finding a partner, or the thing fails miserably. The fist bump offerer issues a challenge to the offeree. Are you man enough to knock knuckles with me? If your timing's even the slightest bit off, your pinkie knuckle goes in first, connecting with the offerer's index knuckle.

I'm a classic handshake guy. I prefer the commitment, the bond of the classic shake with the quick nod and the sharp look right in the eye. There's something poetic about a strong handshake with a guy who's just hit a homer. Ruth and Gehrig didn't do a front-back-slap with a pull back and an index finger pointed to the heavens. Or an elbow bash thing. They shook hands. If Lou was on his way to the plate after the Babe went deep, they'd grip right hands briefly as their paths crossed.

Not everyone feels that way, though. Their attention spans are short. They feel constrained by the classic shake. They don't want to be tied down to one shaker when other prospects are nearby. Hey, love is all around.

Every player's entitled to his preference. But the trouble starts when handshakes get mixed.

Immediately following events that warrant some kind of physical acknowledgment, two players will simultaneously offer handshakes.

125

Let's say I offer the Classic, but Abbott offers the fist. The result is somewhere between a rock-paper-scissors shootout and a freeway smashup.

It all happens very quickly. As my extended hand heads straight for Scott's knuckles, we each realize the mismatch and switch in midair. Then, seeing one another switch, we each panic and start to switch back. But it's too late. Our flaccid hands collapse together in a gesture that has no meaning except awkwardness. We can't undo it. And we can't go back and do it again, just to get it right. The act is uncomfortable and utterly unsatisfying. It's like clumsy sex. Nobody feels good about it. Let's forget it.

It all started so innocently. We thought we could connect. But ultimately, this failed attempt at a bond just widens the gap between us.

We won today, but we shouldn't have. We beat the Kings 9–6, bless their hearts. If ever there was a week to play a team you're sure to beat, it was this week. But we played tentative and we made a lot of mistakes after having two of our last three games rained out. There's a difference between rested and rusty.

And anyway, the Kings have gotten a lot better since the first week of the season. Their 1–6 record is hard to believe. Fiore, their hunky sportscaster rookie seems to have taken control of the team. He's repositioning outfielders, talking to pitchers — a regular team leader. They don't get discouraged, never yell at each other. If the A's were 1–6, we'd completely combust.

I handled a couple of routine plays against the Kings. I got a solid base hit. Scored a couple runs.

No matter how much sense it makes to wait for the right pitch to hit, it's a constant struggle for me. My instinct, and maybe every hitter's instinct, is to walk up there and start hacking. Between at-bats, I pay attention to the other team's pitcher and their defense. I try to watch for patterns the pitcher might get into and think logically about how he might pitch me, given where I'm hitting in the order and who's up after me.

All great strategies, those. Until I'm in the on-deck circle and it's all lost. Millions of years of human evolution, out the window. Thoughtful strategy gives way to caveman club swinging. If the first pitch is in the same hemisphere as home plate, the very core of my being is compelled to swing from the bottoms of my feet. I can't imagine how many hits that costs me every year.

When I resist the temptation to chase anything close, as I have for the past few games, I feel like I'm a pretty good hitter, at least good enough to accomplish whatever the situation calls for. A fly ball, a grounder behind the runner, maybe even a base hit. But the hardest at-bat for me is leading off an inning.

When Johnny Carson ran out of show because he spent too much time flirting with Angie Dickenson, he always apologized at the end and asked the last guest to come back tomorrow night. And the guest always did come back, though I always imagined that some of the thrill of being on the show would be gone. The guest scheduled for the show's last slot, usually an author or some rube from small-town America who played the kazoo or something, was probably pissed off for having to stay another night. Like Johnny's hard-on for Police Woman was more important than the guest's time.

Most times when you lead off an inning, you were left in the on-deck circle the inning before, like that guest on Johnny Carson. The rest of the team is still getting settled from being out in the field on defense. They're digging water bottles out of coolers, they're talking about the plays they made during the last half inning. They're not watching you. You have to supply your own momentum. And there are no runners to move up, no sacrifices to lay down. Your only job is to get on base.

I led off the fifth inning against the Kings today with maybe my best at bat of the season. We were ahead 2–1, though our lead should have been much bigger. Watching the Kings pitcher warm up between innings, I was determined to work the count in my favor and get on base one way or another.

Holding my bat in front of me with both hands, samurai style, I walked behind the umpire, who was bent over, ass in the air, dusting off home plate. I took a few practice swings while looking at Joe coaching third base. He gave me a whole slate-full of obvious decoy signals and clapped his hands twice. All those fake signals can be distracting. But I nodded at him, just for appearances. Digging my back foot into the box, I'd already decided I wasn't going to swing until I had one strike in the count. The Kings' pitcher got a sign he liked from his catcher and started his windup. He threw an overhand fastball that just missed the outside edge of the plate. Ball one. I stepped out and figured he threw me a fastball away because he knew I liked to swing early in the count. It was a pitch I wasn't likely to hit hard.

The next pitch was another fastball away, in virtually the same spot as the last pitch. "Steee-rike one!" Mike the umpire yelled. I peeked back at him and he knew immediately that I thought he'd missed the call. "Outside corner, Pat," Mike said, insistently. "That's a nice pitch."

"OK, Mike," I said without looking at him, even though I disagreed with him. "Don't get excited." Unless the call is particularly terrible or it's one in a series of bad calls, I don't argue with umpires. A lot of players in the league hassle the umpires nonstop. I just can't imagine that does them any good. If I'm worried about the umpires, I'm too distracted to do anything else.

I stepped out and spit into my batting glove and rubbed the stickiness up and down the bat handle. Baseball is the only place in the world where you can gain a small advantage by spitting on yourself.

Even riding a hot streak, I don't have the kind of confidence it takes to look at strike two. With the count at one ball and one strike, I was ready to swing if the pitch looked like it might be where I like it. Careful not to try to guess what kind of pitch was coming — though I suspected I'd see a curveball — I dug in again. The pitcher shook off a sign from the catcher. The next one, he liked. The windup, the pitch. A curveball low and away. I leaned a little in the direction of the pitch as it crossed the plate and had to stop myself from swinging. Ball two.

If the pitcher and catcher were paying attention, and it looked like they were, they'd easily see that I was severely tempted by the last pitch. I nearly bit on that breaking ball. It looked like it might hang in front of me just long enough to get a good swing at. But at the very last instant, it took a sharp dive right under where my swing would've been. Glad I held up.

This time, I didn't step out of the box between pitches. I tapped the rubber end of the metal bat on home plate and got back into my stance. The pitcher was ready quickly too. At two balls and one strike, I knew a fatass fastball was coming. I shifted my weight a little more toward my back foot, to better uncork my biggest swing. After a particularly earnest windup, the pitcher let fly and there it was — like a birthday present, wrapped and sent with love — my favorite pitch. Hell, everybody's favorite pitch. I started my swing, turning my hips to get every ounce of my considerable weight into it. And as soon as I did, I realized I'd been had. This was no fastball. The Kings' pitcher had summoned the nerve to throw me a 2–1 changeup. And like the biggest, dumbest fish in the pond, I took the bait. By the time the pitch, which looked like a balloon, got to home plate, my mighty swing was already spent, my weight completely on my front foot. I got a tiny piece of the pitch and was lucky to tap it foul, the ball hopping harmlessly toward our first base coach.

Two balls and two strikes. I stepped out of the box and looked down at the ground while the pitcher rubbed up a new ball. No more guessing. My wrong guess that he would throw me the fastball had totally changed the momentum of the at-bat. Advantage: pitcher.

I choked up a little as I always do when I'm behind in the count. The two-two pitch was another change, this time down and in. I dropped my hands toward the ball and ripped the pitch foul, again toward the first base coach. He let this one go and a couple of kids in the bleachers raced down the right field line after the foul ball.

By now, the A's bench was paying attention. The at-bat was lasting long enough that guys were settled into their places on the bench. A couple guys chattered the meaningless encouragement meant only to fill space. "Hey hey now. Let's go big man. Way to protect. Let's get 'er going. Start us off."

As the kids chased the foul ball down the line, the pitcher had a look on his face that said he knew he'd gotten away with something. That's when I knew I wouldn't see another inside pitch all day.

Sure enough, the second two-two pitch was a changeup outside. I laid off and the count went full.

The advantage shifted back to me. The pitcher knew that I'd probably get a bat on anything he threw over the plate, especially after the foul ball I just crushed. And he knew I was in a mood to be patient.

The A's bench was fully engaged. "Good A.B! Good A.B! Way to make him work. You got him right where you want him! Make it be there!"

Pitchers almost always hate to walk batters. But walking the guy who's leading off the inning almost always leads to trouble. The team at bat has so many options with a runner at first and nobody out. Even if that runner is as slow as I am.

I kept my back foot planted and stepped my right foot out of the box, pushing my helmet down on my head. The Kings pitcher and I stared at each other while I tightened my batting glove. I stepped back in. He nodded at his catcher and wound up. Big kick. Overhand fastball. Not even close. High and away. "Nope," Mike the umpire said. "Ball four."

Drawing a walk isn't always satisfying. But this time it was. Working the count and protecting the plate with two strikes, a walk accomplished two important things. First — and most obvious — it put a runner on base with no outs in a close game. Second, it forced the pitcher to throw more pitches than he wanted. And if it sapped him of a little confidence along the way, so much the better.

The guys behind me in the batting order also made the pitcher work. It's contagious. One guy sees the benefit and he's got to do it too. Pretty soon, every hitter is waiting for his favorite pitch to hit. Our patience at the plate unlocked the game and led to nine runs.

Me and Jose Bautista were two guys who worked at the same place. We were about the same age. We were interested in many of the same things. Both of us were kind of new to the company. There were far more similarities than differences between us.

But the differences were significant. For one, I earned $3.35 per hour as an employee of the Baltimore Orioles American League Base Ball Club, as our paychecks referred to the organization. Jose Bautista made considerably more than that as a rookie right-handed starter.

The other major difference between between Jose Bautista and me was language. He grew up in Bani, Dominican Republic. I grew up in Raleigh, North Carolina. I'd flailed around in Spanish classes in school and my grasp of the language was limited to asking where I could find a toilet. If I'm only allowed one question in a language, "where is the toilet" isn't a bad place to begin. Once, in Monterrey, Mexico I actually used my Spanish sentence. (*"?Donde esta' el bano?"*) And boy was I glad I did. But a sentence is not a conversation. Especially a question. Especially that question. The question itself implies a powerful desire — a need, even — to get away from the listener, not to mention the listener's desire to get away from the asker. Once the listener points the asker in the direction of a toilet, that's the end of the exchange. Thus, I could have no conversation in Spanish with Jose Bautista.

Which left, if we were to converse at all, his English. Jose Bautista was drafted in 1981 by the New York Mets. He spent seven seasons in the Mets minor league system before the Orioles acquired him the Rule V draft. He made his big league debut with the Orioles in 1988, where he quickly earned the nickname "Boom Boom," thanks to his habit of surrendering long home runs.

Bautista's presence in the starting rotation said a lot about the state of the Orioles organization. A Rule V guy who, in seven years, couldn't crack the Mets pitching staff was suddenly a number three starter in Baltimore. And of course, the years when Bautista waited for a call from the big club were the Mets' glory years. Thus, Bautista could be forgiven for his mopiness around Memorial Stadium.

One late summer Sunday, the day after Boom Boom Bautista had absorbed another ugly loss, he leaned against the fence in the Orioles bullpen watching his teammates warm up. Because he'd pitched the night before, he wasn't required to take part. I finished whatever pregame bullpen task I'd been assigned and stood in the sweltering heat next to Bautista. We rested against the outfield fence, peering through the scratched plastic window at Bautista's teammates taking batting practice.

His hair was a style of the time — the gheri curl: shiny wet locks that required all sorts of oil and who knows what else. Bautista's whole look was, of course, topped with a wool Orioles hat. With the temperature in the 90s and humidity to match, Bautista's gheri curl was in danger of melting all over his uniform. His slippery hair dripped and he smelled like a coconut pie. Bautista's mood was worse than usual.

I greeted Jose. "What's up?"

He didn't look up. A second or two later, he nodded, acknowledging my greeting with the least possible exertion.

"Tough one last night," I said.

A long pause. "Yes. Tough." He swatted halfheartedly at a small cloud of gnats swirling around his head.

"I thought your stuff looked good," I told him, as if it would matter to the starting pitcher that a grounds crew guy thought his stuff looked good.

Bautista waited a long time, then shrugged. "It no that good. But what the fuck?" As is common, Bautista had mastered our language's swear words before he'd mastered syntax. "Fuck it," he declared, spitting a sunflower seed hull against the wall.

I'm not a mind-reader, but I would've sworn at that moment that Jose Bautista was standing in the bullpen, sweating his gheri curl off, wondering how he'd wound up on this team. The Orioles were buried in the standings, he was struggling and baseball season looked like it might never end.

Bautista's body language suggested he wasn't in the mood to chat. So we stood together for a long time, sweating in the sun, silently watching batting practice. He continued to battle the gnats. The gnats were winning.

"Goddamn ants," he muttered.

The game was moving along exactly the way Kings-A's games always do — we score a lot of runs early and play loose for the rest of the day. The competition is friendly and players from each team respect one another. Really, it was just fun.

And then Alex broke his right hand.

There was a collision at first base. A base runner barreled down the first base line, Tim Gaudet scooped up a ground ball at shortstop and threw to first. He sidearmed his throw a little and the ball drifted to the right, in the direction of the steaming base runner. Rather than cut his losses by taking his foot off the bag and trying to prevent the ball from sailing completely off the field, Alex gambled. Left foot still touching the bag, Alex stretched to catch the tailing ball.

The ball and the locomotive of a base runner arrived at the same instant. The runner plowed right into him. At impact, I heard a sharp, staccato smack, like the noise someone makes when they belly flop into a swimming pool. Alex was hit so hard his body moved right out from under his green A's hat which, like a cartoon, seemed to hang suspended in the air for a half second before falling to the ground in a little cloud of dust. Alex's hat rested alone against first base.

Just after the collision, Alex himself made a frightening noise, like a whimper. He rolled around in the dirt, cradling his wrist to his chest. I watched from third base as a crowd gathered around Alex, who suddenly looked a lot older. I stayed at my position and kicked at the dirt a little. It was hard to see Alex in that much pain.

When the half inning was over, Alex was sitting on the bench, trying to flex the fingers on his right hand. He studied the back of his hand and wrist carefully. He showed it to anyone who wanted to see it. There it was, Alex's obviously broken hand, attached to a probably broken wrist. I offered him some ice from a cooler I brought. Alex declined, choosing instead to continue studying his lumpy arm and hand.

Alex stayed on the bench for the rest of the game, but he wasn't happy about it. Over-30 League rules allowed players to sit for an inning or two and re-enter the game. Alex stuck around to see if maybe he could shake it off and get one more at bat, as if the Holy Spirit might visit him and heal his broken bones.

He was gone the next week and the week after that. Often, when a player gets injured and can't play, he'll come out and root his teammates on. Not Alex. Nothing personal, but there was absolutely no way Alex Bell was coming to Orchard Park ballfield without a uniform and a bag full of pharmaceuticals. He couldn't sit and watch.

In addition to being a generally affable bunch of ballplayers, the Kings have one of the most popular players in the league at second base. He's extraordinarily tough, but he's not very good. He's very short and he's very slow. He gets hit by a lot of pitches. He's not even very friendly, really.

But he's an orthopedic surgeon who specializes in arthroscopic knee and shoulder surgeries. John "Doc" Martin has 'scoped dozens of players in the Over-30 League. Last season, he drove a needle full of cortisone so far into Joe Sorenson's shoulder joint that the hulking Athletic cried. "It hurt worse than anything I've ever experienced," Joe said. "It hurt so bad it made me sick." But Doc Martin saved the rest of Joe's season.

Doc doesn't care who you play for. If you're in the Over-30 League, he'll gladly accept your case. He understands the mechanics and the physics of elbows, shoulders and knees, and how fragile joints get abused on a baseball diamond.

A year or two ago, Doc Martin reassembled Tim Gaudet's shoulder. Tim pitched the last two months of a season in severe pain. Every pitch he threw brought tears to his eyes. Finally, and long after he should have, he had to stop pitching. That winter, Doc Martin went into Tim's right shoulder and had a look around. The main problem was a torn labrum and frayed rotator cuff, but Tim said Doc found all kinds of junk in there. He cleaned house and tidied up the inside of Tim's shoulder. After he sat out much of the next season, Tim's been as good as new since.

I've been lucky. The only serious injuries I've sustained since coming back to baseball have been a couple of broken fingers. Both happened when I was catching. The first broken finger was a fluke foul tip that hit me square on the back of my left thumb, inside my catcher's mitt. It hurt like hell, but the second one hurt a lot worse.

Kevin O'Hare was pitching and was a little more pissed off than usual. When Kevin has control trouble on the mound, he compounds the problem by getting furious, first at himself, then at anyone who dares try to calm him down.

He walked the first two batters he faced that day. I was trying to mix up his pitches, calling for lots of breaking balls, both as a way to accent Kevin's overpowering fastball and help him retain his confidence by showing him I believed he could still get his curveball over the plate. See what you have to do when you're a catcher?

Kevin's next curveball arced high in the air and floated down and in to the left-handed batter, who raked it into right field for an RBI single. Kevin watched the ball fall in front of our right fielder. He put his glove over his face and screamed, "Fuck!" With runners on first and third and no outs, I asked the umpire for time out and walked toward the mound to talk to Kevin, to settle him down and discuss the next hitter.

"Turn around and get back behind that fucking plate," Kevin growled when he saw me heading in his direction. He narrowed his eyes and pointed a finger at me. "Don't fucking come out here and tell me to calm down. I mean it. I'll rip your head off."

If I obliged his unreasonable demand, I was admitting I wasn't in control. And the catcher's always got to be in control. But if I finished walking to the mound, my pitcher might really rip my head off. I straightened my catcher's mask and kept walking. I told myself not to tell Kevin to calm down. When somebody's in a hysterical rage, the last thing they want to hear is "calm down." That's the whole point of hysteria, isn't it? The inability to calm down. Kevin embraced his hysteria. "Goddammit, Pat, I told you! Get the fuck away from me!" Kevin was shouting now, not bothering to cover his mouth with his mitt. He didn't care who heard it. He was more angry at himself than he was at me. But he was still pretty angry at me, too. "I can't fucking get anybody in this sorry-ass league out! And nothing you tell me is going to change that! So get the fuck out of here!"

Just to make a point, I told him he still looked strong, he was spotting his fastball well and that we should mix in a couple of off-speed pitches to keep the next hitter off balance. "Fuck you!" Kevin yelled at me. "Get out of here!"

A catcher can only take so much and I'd reached my own boiling point. Now I was mad. "Aw, Kevin," I said walking back to home plate. "Why don't you just fucking calm down?"

He was mad enough to kill me. But when Kevin gets in his moods where no one can talk him out of his despair, it can have an effect on the whole team.

When I returned to home plate after my unsuccessful conference, the umpire asked me what I'd said to Kevin. "Hey, nice work," the umpire said. "He looks more pissed off than when you went out there. You should be a shrink."

I was in no mood. "Yeah, well. Just don't get too comfortable back here." Kevin was so mad that he was likely to throw the ball so hard that he had no control. Throwing as a way of expressing anger, rather than pitching with the goal of retiring batters.

"I'll try to block whatever he throws," I told the umpire. "But I'm not making any promises."

"Aw Christ." he said. "OK. Play ball."

Kevin and I managed to get a one ball, two strike count on the batter, who looked overmatched against Kevin's smoking fastball. The umpire had been right: Kevin was throwing with every ounce of strength in his big body. But he was throwing strikes, which surprised me, the umpire and the batter, who heard my conversation with the umpire and was terrified he'd take one in the ribs. Nevertheless, strikes or no strikes, Kevin continued to seethe on the mound. Quick-pitching, he barely looked at me when I gave him the signs. He started his windup before I was even set. With the count one and two, I signaled for a curveball. Before I had a chance to set up on the outside half of the plate, Kevin went into his violent windup. With a runner at third, I couldn't afford a passed ball, so I was poised to pounce on anything in the dirt. Kevin's pitch came out of his hand and was headed for the heart of the plate. Since it was a curveball, it would dive low and outside. Though my feet weren't set, I thought I had a chance to block the curveball in the dirt.

Only it wasn't a curveball. Kevin had ignored my sign and thrown a fastball. The ball, of course, didn't break. But my finger did. I had my right arm in front of me, expecting to block a pitch in the dirt. And since the pitch was straight as a string, I was in a weird position to catch it. Off balance, I tried to gather the pitch in with both hands and it hit me square on the end of the right index finger. For the first 10 or 20 seconds, the pain was blinding. I have no idea what I did. But when I finally opened my eyes, I was on my knees near the on-deck circle, bent forward like I was praying to Mecca.

The broken finger happened fairly early in the season, so I did manage to make it back for the last five or six games of the year. Kevin at least pretended to feel bad about it.

136

Eleven

When I was in the eighth grade, the unthinkable happened.

For some reason, a long list of the biggest stars in Major League Baseball descended on my little hometown for some kind of banquet honoring Pete Rose. It was November, only a month after Rose's Phillies won the World Series against Kansas City.

My dad told me the Saturday night banquet wasn't for kids — "Language," he said, shaking his head — but I learned that the big leaguers would conduct a clinic for kids during the day. And, as a bonus, a sort of kickoff to my big league weekend, Pete Rose himself would be at the Best Products store on Friday afternoon on my side of town. Pete would be signing autographs after school from three to five. My sister and I would have to ride a different bus to get to the Western Boulevard Best Products, but I figured if we didn't mess around after school like we usually did, we'd make it in time to get Pete's autograph.

My younger sister, of course, didn't care about baseball. She didn't even bother to actively dislike it. She just didn't care about it. But it was rare that anybody as famous as Pete Rose came to Raleigh, so she went along with the Best Products plan.

When the afternoon school bell rang, Kelly and I shot out of Sacred Heart Cathedral and, as if by a miracle, the number 12 bus was sitting there waiting for us. Sometimes when things are right, you just know everything's going to be OK. The bus was nearly empty when we got on. Maybe two or three riders got on and off between our downtown school and our stop, right in front of the department store. Kelly and I ran down the bus steps and sprinted across the store's parking lot, weaving between parked cars. We got to the sidewalk and stomped on the black rubber mat outside the automatic doors of Best Products.

We waited an extra second for them to slide apart. And then we saw the line. Rather, we saw the back of the line. Pete was rumored to be at the other end of the massive department store, at a table signing autographs. It looked like we'd never get to the front of the line by five o'clock.

But a little bit at a time, the line moved. I'd brought along several copies of Sport Magazine, the issues that covered the Phillies in the World Series. I had some other glossy pictures of Rose that I gave Kelly, so she'd have something for him to sign. There was the famous picture of Rose during his days with Cincinnati, sliding headfirst into third during the 1975 Series against Boston, his helmet flying off his head. And the All-Star Game home plate collision with Ray Fosse. And a couple of Rose's Topps baseball cards. I didn't expect him to autograph all of them, just whichever one he liked best. Then, maybe we could chat for a minute about the picture and why he liked it.

While we waited in line, I explained to Kelly that I really was conflicted about all this. After all, we were a Pirates family. We'd get Pete Rose's autograph, but we'd still be Pirates fans.

We waited and the line slowed. People packed closer together, craning their necks to see if maybe Pete Rose was within sight. The line wound up and down the aisles of the store. Fishing rods, household products, electronics.

"Hey, look," Kelly said. "Look who's here." She pointed at a smiling, charging herd of nuns. "What are they doing here?"

Six nuns from our school were dressed in full nun regalia, black habits with no hair showing. Just their sweaty pink faces peeking out of the contraptions they wore on their heads. They belonged to an order of missionaries, meant to convert the heathens to Catholicism. They were all from Philadelphia, apparently the Nun Capital of America. Since there weren't many Catholics in North Carolina, these nuns chose to do their missionary work in Raleigh.

"Dammit," I whispered. "They're going to cut in line! Watch! They're going to walk right past us and get right up next to Pete Rose!"

Naturally, they were Phillies fans, nun Phillies fans who were, at this moment, jumping right to the front of the endless line. While the rest of us struggled in Purgatory, patiently awaiting our final reward,

God's robed servants zoomed past Kelly and me — though I was certain they saw us — and got shiny new baseballs signed by Pete Rose. Probably had their pictures taken, too. People can't get enough of that. Nuns doing this, nuns doing that. Nuns sitting next to Pete Rose.

The line had moved about three feet since the nuns blew past us. Now they blew past us again, this time in the other direction, turning the baseballs over in their hands, examining Pete Rose's signature. Their habits flapping behind them, they glided through the automatic doors, back to the convent.

When we finally got within sight of Pete Rose — "There he is!" Kelly said — a pasty man with short sleeves and a fat necktie who worked at Best Products saw all the stuff we'd brought for Pete to sign, the pictures and magazines and baseball cards. "Y'all kids can't bring that up here," the man twanged. "Mr. Rose will not sign them. You must purchase a Best Brand baseball. That is the only item being autographed today."

"But... but... bu... buh... buh huh huh huh huh!" My sister exploded into sobs. "Weeee... weeee... weeee don't have any moooooooney! Buh huh huh huh huh!"

Kelly was right. And even if we did have money, we'd have to get out of line to go get baseballs and we'd never make it back in time. "I'm sorry, y'all will have to leave," the Best man said. By now, I was ready to tell the Best Products guy and Pete Rose to kiss my ass. But suddenly Pete Rose meant something to my sister. We'd waited all this time, we'd hurried here from school.

"Don't cry, Kell," I told her. "Like I said, we're Pirates fans anyway. Who needs this creepy store?"

"But Pat, you want it! It's for you!" She had ahold of the front of my white Catholic school oxford with both hands. "We gotta get it! He'll never be back!"

While Kelly was crying, some kind souls who were behind us in line appeared with a little paper bag.

"Here, you two," a woman said. "It's OK. You stay."

"Thank you," Kelly said red-faced and puffy from crying, looking up at the woman. I didn't really know which was more embarrassing — Kelly's bawling or being the target of a stranger's charity. When

139

it finally was our turn in line, I was pretty disgusted with the whole thing. Still, here was Pete Rose, right in front of me.

"Hi, Mr. Rose," I said, handing him my baseball. "Congratulations on the World Series. Welcome to Raleigh. We don't get many blah blah blah..." I jabbered at Rose while he sullenly signed my ball. He didn't respond. When he was done with my ball, he rolled it across the table toward me.

Kelly was next. She silently held out her baseball, not nearly close enough for Rose to reach.

"Well, hello there, sweetheart," Pete gushed to my sister. "What's your name?"

"Kelly," she whispered.

"What's that honey?" Pete Rose stood up and leaned far over the table, taking the ball from my sister's hand. "Can't hear you. Speak up."

I hollered. "KELLY! HER NAME'S KELLY! I'M HER BROTHER!"

Rose ignored me. "Thanks for coming today, Kelly. Are you a baseball fan?"

The next day, my dad dropped me off at a convention-type hotel ballroom in north Raleigh and I went in for the clinic. Rose's Philadelphia infield mates Larry Bowa and Mike Schmidt were there. Phillie centerfielder Garry Maddox was there. One of my three favorite players of all time Willie Stargell was there. But when I walked into the huge hotel ballroom, I didn't see any of them. What I saw was a giant man in a tiny chair, the kind of little plastic-backed chair you see in an elementary school. The man wasn't so much sitting on the chair as he was laying across it. His long legs stretched out in front of him, crossed at the ankles. His hands rested on the floor, beneath the miniature chair. I took a couple steps closer and looked at him. Dave Kingman. It's King Kong Kingman. Wearing faded Levi's and a golf shirt, slouched in a chair, looking like Gulliver. I didn't say anything to the famously crabby Kingman. I just sort of looked.

He looked up at me, confused.

"Hey, what time is it?" Kingman asked me.

"Umm... I don't know. About one o'clock, probably. The clinic starts at one."

"Shit. I gotta get something to eat," King Kong said. "Where's the food?"

"Uh..."

"Fuck it. I'll find it."

Dave Kingman untwisted his legs and stood up from the little chair. He stretched like he'd just gotten out of bed and gave me a little slap on the head before he walked away in search of lunch.

You'd think a 6–1 record would make a team feel confident. The only game we've lost all season was to last year's league champions. But the A's do not feel confident. With three of the first ten games rained out, we've had trouble staying in a rhythm. Worse, those rainouts came against good teams. Makeup games against the toughest teams in the league are going to get stacked one after another at the end of the season.

We're the shakiest 6–1 team you've ever seen. In addition to Alex's injury, we lost Scott Abbott. Well, not all of him. Just his pitching arm. Scott, it seems, returned home from work one rainy evening this week to find his wet dog sleeping on the living room couch. The dog ignored his master's call to get his wet self off the furniture. Scott angrily lifted the dog off the couch and gave the pooch a toss. With his right arm. When non-ballplayers do things like this, even non-ballplayers who don't have particularly strong arms and shoulders, nothing happens. But because baseball players, pitchers in particular, put such a strain on their arms, they're more likely to get injured in day-to-day household activities. Like dog-throwing. Something happened in Scott's shoulder when he tossed his wet dog off the couch. A pop, a crunch, a groan. The dog was fine. The pitcher was not fine.

"What the hell happened?" Joe asked when Scott told him he pJoeably couldn't pitch.

"I threw my dog," Scott said. There was no good way to say it. "I picked him up and heaved him and something in my shoulder went out."

"Went out? Out where?" Joe knew exactly what Abbott meant.

"Just out," Scott moped. "I threw my dog and I threw my shoulder with him."

141

"How big is your dog?"

"Eighty or ninety pounds, I guess," Scott said. "He's a lab."

Joe was disgusted. He turned his head, spit and winced. "Fatass dog."

So Tim Gaudet started against the Pilots. And after a seven-run first inning, he was just fine. Actually, Tim never made it past the two-out mark of the first. DD brought in Rod Clement to soak up the mess. A lot can happen in a seven-run inning. There were cheap hits, legitimate hits, walks, errors, missed cutoff men and swinging bunts. Guys hit good pitches, bad pitches, pitches meant to be wasted. After an inning and a third, the Pilots lead was 11–1.

Naturally, that's when the A's relaxed. With nothing on the line, players thought only of their batting averages and RBI totals. Clement cruised through his innings and Lance Blake pitched the end of the game. We inched back a little at a time. The comeback came up a little short and we lost 11–10.

The comeback should have been uplifting. We should have hollered, "This team never quits!" But we didn't. Instead, the ugly mojo that follows Pilots games hung in the air like smoke.

You could tell during our comeback that something wasn't right. Nobody was kidding around, nobody even bothered to hoot at the umpire when he missed a call.

Our next game was against the Bulls. The Bulls are tough every year. They're exactly the wrong team to face when you're wobbly.

Unlike the last couple weeks, the weather for the game against the Bulls was absolutely perfect. Sunny, clear, not too hot, a little breeze. Perfect weather for anything, but especially perfect baseball weather. When the weather's nice, fans come to the Over-30 League games. They're all related to the players, of course. But still.

There are the regulars. Julie, of course, hasn't missed many A's games over the years. Whether to watch Abbott or Joe, she's been here. My wife shows up most weeks with our dog Lucy in tow. Lance's wife and baby son come to some of the games. But this week, this weather, brings fans out of the woodwork.

Among those fans are Jack Richmond's family. Jack has gotten no better over the course of the season. He can't hit and he can't field. He can pitch a little. But only a little. Since he joined the team last year, Jack's been a mystery. All we know is that he's some kind of accountant. He doesn't say much and appears to have even less fun than the rest of us.

Today, his family has brought a picnic to the game and is sitting on a hill down the right field line, away from the players and the rest of the fans who sit in bleachers behind the bench. Jack's wife and a couple of small children are sitting on a blanket in the grass. There's a cooler and some nice-looking sandwiches. Matching place settings, even. In folding lawn chairs next to the blanket are Jack's parents.

The A's got off to a hot start. The Bulls didn't have much pitching today and we opened up a 5–0 lead by the third inning.

There are a few unique rules in the Over-30 League. To make sure that everyone gets a chance to play, there's a re-entry rule. That means, if you come out of the game, you're allowed to come back in later. There's also a rule prohibiting pitchers from throwing more than four innings in a game. This is a good idea. There are so few really good pitchers in our league that managers would ruin pitchers' arms in the first couple weeks of the season.

Clement started the game against the Bulls and pitched four scoreless innings. He totally shut down a big-hitting team. While we were batting in the bottom of the fourth, DD told Jack Richmond to get loose. He would pitch the fifth. Our half of the inning didn't last long. The new Bulls pitcher threw only soft breaking balls and induced an inning-ending double play. Richmond was in the game.

DD put CJ Demakis at third for an inning and I watched the infielders from the bench while Jack warmed up. Jack threw hard. But he was all over the place, throwing pitches in the dirt or all the way to the backstop. I knew the team wasn't very confident in Richmond to begin with. And his warm-up pitches only made things worse.

The first batter stepped to the plate and stood in the batter's box. Jack Richmond looked in at Kevin O'Hare for the sign.

"C'mon, Jack!," "Go get 'em Jack!," "You can do it Jack!" and "Yay Daddy!" poured down the right field line from the Richmond family picnic. Richmond went into his slow windup and fired his first pitch directly into the ribs of the right-handed batter. The ball made a thump when it hit the batter's body, as if it struck a melon. The batter fell to his knees and doubled over in pain, gulping for air. Richmond said nothing, just waited, glove in the air, for the catcher to throw him a new ball. Coughing, the batter recovered his breath and walked to first base.

The Richmond family was not discouraged. "That's OK, Jack!," "Hey, how about a double play?," "No harm done, Jack!," "Get the next guy, Dad!"

Jack adjusted his glasses, rubbed up the baseball and went into his stretch as the next hitter dug in. Bent at the waist, Jack looked over his left shoulder at the base runner who was still holding his ribs. Jack came to a set position and paused. The runner didn't move. Jack kicked and delivered his next pitch, another fastball, squarely into the batter's midsection. His ribs also made a noise like a melon. Maybe that's just what it sounds like when a guy takes a fastball in the ribs.

The Richmond family fell silent.

The Bulls leapt from their bench and quickly took a few menacing steps onto the field. They berated Jack, swearing at him and accusing him of throwing at their players. A couple of their guys came out to help the injured player, who lay flat on his back, gasping audibly to recover the oxygen Jack's pitch had displaced from his lungs. The home plate umpire removed his mask and somehow convinced the Bulls not to form a dogpile on the A's pitcher. When the Bulls were settled down, he walked toward the mound and theatrically issued Jack a warning. One more hit batter and he was gone. Did he understand that? Jack stood slack on the mound, expressionless, nodding.

But the Bulls knew, the umpire knew, the A's knew. We all knew Jack wasn't throwing at these batters. He was nervous. His family was watching. His dad was watching. The only thing worse than playing badly is playing badly in front of someone who's come to watch you play. And the only thing worse than that is when your dad is at the game.

DD got up from the bench and, before visiting Jack on the mound, told Lance to get loose. I grabbed a catcher's mitt and mask and trotted down the line to the bullpen. While Lance windmilled his arm to get blood flowing before he started warming up, I watched Jack and DD argue on the mound. Jack made it clear that he didn't appreciate the visit from the manager. Before DD was done talking to him, Jack turned his back and rubbed up the baseball.

Jack Richmond's dad was standing in front of his lawn chair now. Jack's wife was gathering up the picnic food. Their day was ruined. And it would get worse.

The next batter walked. The one after that smashed a double to the wall. The next guy singled. Four runs in, no outs recorded.

DD took two steps off the bench and signaled to the umpire that he was making a pitching change. Jack was beside himself. "No! Goddammit, you are not taking me out of this game," Jack yelled at DD. The manager arrived at the mound and held out his hand, silently demanding that Jack hand over the ball. "Nuh-uh! I am not coming out of this game!" Jack jabbed his finger an inch from DD's nose. "This is bullshit, DD! You *know* it's bullshit!"

From the bullpen, I wondered what Jack meant. He couldn't possibly think he was being lifted unfairly, could he? Finally, after more dramatics, he pounded the ball into DD's hand and stomped off the mound.

"This is crap," Jack yelled, throwing his glove at the bench. "I've had it!"

When DD got back to the bench, Jack confronted him. "How can I pitch when you pull me as soon as anything's wrong?"

"Whaddya mean, sonny? You got rocked out there," DD said, laughing incredulously. "It's a one-run game now."

"If that was Scott or Rod or Tim, you'd let them finish the inning," Jack said, red-faced and voice cracking. "I never get to finish an inning."

"Hey, settle down," DD said. Now he was annoyed. "Get 'em next time." Which meant, of course, DD wouldn't be sending old Jack Richmond to the mound again anytime soon. But Jack did the dirty work for him.

"No, DD! There's no next time," Jack screamed. "Fuck you and fuck this team!"

By now, the Richmond family was gathered behind the A's bench, packed up and ready to go. Jack stomped with them up the hill to their cars. Jack got in a car by himself and zoomed away from the ballpark, kicking up gravel and dust in the parking lot. His family followed him.

The carnage continued and we lost 8–5. Never has a beautiful day been ruined so quickly and perfectly.

While nobody would miss Jack Richmond much, his tantrum and his dramatic resignation were unsettling. We all knew how painful it was for Jack to do so poorly in front of his family. Was his freak-out a way to save face in front of them? Were they supposed to think he'd be successful if not for his lousy manager and teammates?

So far, two guys have quit the A's in one year and neither one had the decency to wait until the game — or the inning — was over.

If there was rain within a thousand miles of Baltimore, the grounds crew had to be at the park at dawn on Saturdays and Sundays. During the week, the city paid guys to hang around the stadium and do nothing. But on the weekends, it was up to us. Most grounds crew guys had the same morning routine for these marathon days. Punch the clock. Fall asleep in a chair. One lucky grounds crew guy could secure the musty old naugahyde couch over by the lawn mowers. But the rest of us slept anywhere we could. I discovered that the bullpen shed was a great place to sleep off a Friday night bender. Fast asleep in the bullpen after a particularly late evening of fun, I was startled awake.

"Oh, sorry," a smiling guy said, pulling a running shoe onto his foot. "Didn't mean to wake you. Long night?"

"Uh... yeah. That's OK," I stammered. "No problem."

Weird that a stranger would show up in the bullpen. His threadbare tee shirt and his jogging shorts told me the guy was here for some exercise. Just dropped by Memorial Stadium first thing in the morning to get a sweat going. Should I use the pitchers' phone to call the cops? The guy was clearly getting ready to take a jog around the stadium. What kind of neighborhood loony thought it was OK sneak into the stadium for a run?

"Hey, uh, buddy?" I said to the guy, cracking my neck, which had stiffened during my nap. "You can't do that here." I waved my hand at him, shooing him away. "You gotta leave."

146

"Huh? No, no. It's OK," he said, windmilling his arms, getting ready for a big workout. "Don't worry about it."

I hate when people say that. "I'm not worried about it," I said, a little impatient. "You just can't be here, pal. Let's go. Come with me."

If Schultz saw this nut running around on the field, getting a morning constitutional in, he'd kill him. I was doing the guy a favor by keeping him from a homicidal groundskeeper.

"I don't think so," the guy said. "Just take it easy."

"Look, buddy. I said it nice. Now don't make me get ugly. I'm not gonna ask you again." Now I was starting to getting mad.

The guy took about three steps toward me and I read his ratty old T-shirt. "Milwaukee Brewers," it said. "Why don't you just calm down, kid? I'm the Brewers manager. All I want to do is run some laps around the warning track. Don't get excited."

Tom Treblehorn didn't look a thing like a big league manager. He was slim and friendly. And he wasn't wearing a baseball uniform. I was mortified. But more than that, I was worried for my job. Surely, Treblehorn would tell somebody that the grounds crew guy in the bullpen dared hassle a major league manager and needed to be an ex-grounds crew guy in a hurry. "Jeez, sorry Mr. Treblehorn. I didn't realize it was you."

"Hey, that's OK," the manager said. "No harm done. Go back to your nap."

Lance's been talking for a long time about defecting to another team next season.

"This is bullshit," he whispered to me last week. "DD's not running this team. Joe is."

"Everybody knows that," I told him. Some players have questioned why DD bothers to maintain the charade of managing the team when his stepson clearly makes the decisions. "What's your point?"

"The point is, there's no leadership. Like signs — look at our signs. Everybody in the league knows our signs."

"What? No they don't. Nobody cares about our signs."

"Like hell! Look at the bunt you put down today."

I had to admit, I did lay down a perfect bunt that day that the third baseman was in perfect position to field.

"As soon as DD gave you that bunt sign, the third baseman moved in 15 feet. What the hell is that?"

Lance had been pestering Joe and DD to change the signals all season. But since they had such trouble remembering the signs as they were, they refused to come up with new ones.

Lance said, "The only thing that keeps other teams is guessing is that our guys miss so many signs. The other teams know them better than we do."

That was probably true. The A's were as likely to miss a sign as they were to heed one. Maybe one out of five or six signs actually produced what it was supposed to. That bothered Lance, who was a weird mix of clowning around and discipline. He believed baseball was to be played and managed a certain way and that the A's neither played nor were managed that way.

"I've had it with this team," he told me. "I'm playing somewhere else next year. The Tigers, probably. You wanna come?"

It didn't make sense to me. "You're going to change teams because you don't like our signs? Jeez, Lance. Seems a little extreme."

"Not just that," he said. "Look at these guys." He pointed to a crowd of A's sprawled in the grass on the hill down the first base line, hats perched on their faces to cover their eyes while they napped before the game. "This team's never gonna win anything."

I tried to imagine myself in an Tigers uniform. I couldn't do it.

"Nah, I'll probably stay here," I told him. I couldn't see myself playing for anyone else. For all our problems, the A's were my team.

After a smoking start, we've lost three straight. Tempers are short. Nobody's laughing. We look desperate. When the team is winning, guys don't mind the new playing arrangement as much. When we're losing, guys who ride the bench a lot start to wonder if maybe they couldn't fail just as easily as the players on the field.

On the other hand, I've been playing like a 19-year-old for the past month. I'm hitting everything hard, driving in runs, making plays at third. When you're hitting well, the ball moves in slow motion.

Whether you're in the field or at the plate, you can anticipate perfectly what the ball's going to do. If it moves a little, you move with it. It seems so easy.

My swing came back and my throwing arm didn't hurt. I was having a great time. But in our second game against the Giants, I came close to having my head removed. Playing in on the grass at third base, guarding against a bunt by the leadoff batter, I made a huge — and dangerous — mistake. I got distracted.

At Orchard Park ballfield, the backdrop for the third baseman is a little parking lot up on a hill. Since ours was the last game of the day, players from the other games hung around to watch us. Some of the Hornets, who'd endured a thrashing in the one o'clock game, were drinking beer out of the back of somebody's truck. They were rowdy and started riding Paul, the overweight, effeminate home plate umpire. Each time Paul would make a call, the drunken Hornets would prance around their beer truck, imitating him. Standing about fifty feet from home plate, I became more interested in the soused Hornets than the hitter. Despite playing way in on the infield grass, I looked past the batter, at the obnoxious Hornets dancing around like monkeys in their filthy uniform pants and undershirts. It was sort of funny, really.

Then the right-handed batter took a full swing at a breaking ball. I suppose he connected, but I never saw it. I never saw anything. I heard a humming noise brush past me and a tiny breeze followed behind it against my right cheek. The ball was past me before I knew it was even hit. Really, another baseball's width to my left and the ball would have broken my face open like an egg. I kicked at the dirt as the left fielder handled the ball on a bounce and threw to Lance at second.

"You okay?" Rod Clement asked from short. "What happened? You didn't move."

"I don't know," I said, shaken. "I just lost it."

"Well, bro, you better fuckin' get it back quick. You can't go to sleep over there. You'll get killed."

"Right," I said, shaking it off. "Right. Killed."

The runner didn't amount to anything. We got out of the inning without further incident.

In my first at-bat of the game, I led off the third inning against

George Bloch. George's a tall, long-armed pitcher who changes speeds and hits his spots. He's probably the best control pitcher in the league. He doesn't throw all that hard, but when he follows a breaking ball or a change-up with a fastball, it's hard to get the bat around in time to do any damage. For me, anyway.

I caught Bloch for a couple innings last year in the all-star game. He dispatched batter after batter in an all-star lineup. Catching him, I learned a little more about the way he pitches. He likes to set batters up, manipulating them and fooling them into thinking they're in charge. Then he exploits the confidence he's given them.

Bloch throws me a first-pitch curveball away and in the dirt. I've already told myself I'm not going to swing at a bad pitch. I tell myself that a lot, but I swing at a lot of bad pitches anyway. This time it works and I lay off. Bloch's next pitch is up and in, spinning me away from the plate, ducking. Considering his control, this is no accident. It's smart pitching. He's trying to make me think twice about hanging out over the plate to reach for a pitch on the outside corner. And of course, that's where his next pitch is. It's a fastball away that looks pretty appetizing. Rather than try to pull the ball to right field — always a temptation for me — I decide to relax a little, swing hard and just put the bat on the ball. I line the ball over the third baseman, slicing it down the left field line. I chug as hard as I can to first base and make a big turn. I act like I'm thinking about second base, but really I'm exhausted.

Eventually, I make it all the way around the bases and score one of three runs we get in the inning. In an unexpected reversal, the Giants turn into the Athletics, making silly mistakes and playing unsure of themselves. We build a 5–1 lead and manage to hold off a furious late rally. They make their last out with the tying run stranded at second. Final score: A's 7, Giants 6.

I've wondered all season which team we really are. Are the A's the big slugging team with three or four good pitchers and terrific team defense? Or are we the lethargic, grouchy team with scatter arms and short attention spans? I'm still not sure. But today's win did something to us. We might slide into the tank next week, but I don't think we'll forget how well we played today and how hard we fought to hang on to this game.

We have no trouble with the Browns the following week. The score was 11–7, but it wasn't nearly that close. Our team is different after the Giants win. We're confident and we're pretty sure we're one of the two or three best teams in the league. But "confident" and "happy" are not synonyms.

Chris Nichols is the latest member of the A's to be unhappy about this year's playing arrangements. "Are you having any fun?" Chris asked me this week while we sat on the bench before the game. "I mean, really having fun like we did the first couple years we played on this team?" Chris and I came into the league together.

"This team's different," I told him. "We're winning. Don't you think that's fun?"

He didn't hesitate. "Not if I'm always on the outs with the team. This team's like a bunch of junior high school kids. In crowd, out crowd." Chris shook his head and kicked at an empty water bottle under the bench. "Who the hell needs it?"

I couldn't disagree with Chris about the cliques on the team. But then, I guess I was a little closer to the in crowd than Chris was.

"At least you have a regular position," Chris continued. "Me? They stick me wherever they can. An inning in right field, an inning at second base. I get no rhythm."

"Well, then say something," I said. "Say something about your playing time to Joe or to DD." I tried to encourage Chris. "You're a clutch hitter. You get the hits when we need them. You can..."

"Ah, the hell with it." Chris waved the idea off. "Hey, Pat. Listen. I appreciate it. But look, I'm not very good. I'm not Abbott or O'Hare or Clement. I just come out here to play a little ball. This is a recreational league, for God's sake. These guys treat it like there's actually something at stake. It's time for me to start playing golf."

Kevin O'Hare has gone into a slump that I don't think he'll make it back from. Kevin is the first guy to try to put other players' successes and failures into perspective. He'll put his huge arm around you after a pop-up or some other maddening failure. "Hey, that's gotta feel good, huh?" he says with a mixture of sarcasm and empathy. "Did you see

151

how high that went? You hit the shit out of that ball! And straight! Man, it went right up the chute."

Then he'll get real quiet and whisper, "Really, it's just the Over-30 League."

But as soon as he hits a fly ball or — god forbid — strikes out, perspective fades from memory completely. Kevin has three stages of failure. First is rage. No matter who's around, he becomes so enraged that it actually feels dangerous to be near him. Next, is rationalization. This isn't baseball. This is a farce. Look at us. We look like idiots. Who told us we could wear baseball uniforms? This is actually pretty insulting to the rest of us, since Kevin is by far the most fit player on the team. When he calls himself a middle-aged fatso, what the hell does that make the rest of us who really are? Finally, in his last stage of failure, Kevin sinks into disconsolate, quiet despair.

It says a lot about the A's that we won today and still aren't having any fun. I brought a cooler full of beer for after the game, but the team scattered as soon as the last out was in the book. Lance's mad at everybody and talks quietly about playing for a different team next year. The players who imagine themselves as team leaders — Joe, Abbott and Kevin — grow further apart from the rest of the team. The insurgents — Chris and Lance — don't much care for one another and approach their insurgency from different directions.

Twelve

In Abbott's first game back from his dog-throwing injury, the Tigers beat us 11–9. This is a game we should have won. We lost because the baseball gods determined we'd gotten too pleased with ourselves. The brief confidence we enjoyed was so foreign that it threw the whole team off. Some teams win with bad mojo. There are teams that feed off negative energy and turn their dislike for one another against their opponents. The major league Oakland Athletics of the 1970s were like that. They hated each other and they created a dynasty.

The Lutherville Athletics aren't like that. We don't play well when we're mad. We should get counseling, is what we should do. Maybe there's a marriage counselor somewhere who would take our case.

For most of the week before the Tigers game, the temperature hung around 95 degrees. The sun pounded on the city day after day. If you've ever been to the mid-Atlantic region of the United States in the summer months, perhaps you have some idea of what this means. The soaking heat is worse than oppressive. It's suffocating. The hot, thick air makes being outdoors miserable. And it makes physical activity nearly unbearable, particularly when you're in the kind of physical condition I'm in. Which is to say, not very good.

I wear these fancy, space-age T-shirts beneath my jersey that are supposed to pull sweat from your body and evaporate it into the air. Poof! No more sweating! Except when the temperature is like this and there's nowhere for the perspiration to go. The air is already saturated with filthy, smelly water. So I sweat twice as hard as I usually do — which is really saying something — and it rolls off my space-age undershirt and right into my pants.

I played a terrible game at third base. I don't know what's happening. It started in infield practice. A couple balls went right through my legs. It's weird, because I've really enjoyed infield practice all season. We've put a little routine together for our pre-game infield drills. The routine involves an elaborate rotation, in which a player will field a ground ball, throw to first and cover his base while the ball zooms around the infield in a complicated pattern, players spinning and throwing. It's impressive when it's working. When it's not, it's dizzying and maybe a little dangerous, balls flying all over the place.

Today, everybody in the infield is fine but me. I don't know, maybe it's the heat. Or my near beheading against the Giants. I'm just not feeling it. Balls are getting by me and I can feel the rest of the team losing confidence in their third baseman, one guy at a time. One ball bounces past me and the whole infield chimes in, encouraging me to stay low, keep my glove on the ground, stay in front of it and other remedies for my ailing glove. As more and more balls hop off my chest or under my glove, I hear fewer and fewer shouts of encouragement. Finally, on a play to my left, a rolling ground ball sneaks under my glove and into the outfield grass. Silence.

When the game starts, I continue to not feel it. I finish the game with three errors — two with the glove and one bizarre throw that sails eight feet over the first baseman's head, like one of those balsa wood gliders. Alex didn't even try to catch it. He just watched it fly over his head and nearly into the woods.

After you make an error, the proper thing to do is appear resolute but contrite. Maybe you acknowledge, just loud enough for the rest of the infield to hear, that the base runner is your fault. Your mates in the infield, on the mound and behind the plate are supposed to want to redeem you, determined to avenge your error. They're not supposed to confirm your admission. "My fault," I said after I missed an easy chance.

"No shit," Abbott muttered from the mound, throwing the rosin bag hard into the dirt. A little white cloud from the bag drifted heavily toward center field. And my last shred of baseball confidence drifted with it.

Like baseball itself, work at baseball stadiums usually involves a lot of standing around, waiting for something to happen. During a long stretch waiting to see whether or not it would rain, I asked the ballpark operations guy about an incident at Memorial Stadium years before.

Angelo was the "ballpark operations" guy at Memorial Stadium. That meant he was sort of the super maintenance man of the stadium.

"Hey, Angelo," I asked him. "Were you here when the plane crashed into the upper deck?"

"Hella yes, I wuzza here," Angelo replied. His viscous Italian accent belied his roots. Angelo was born and raised in Baltimore. But he was from the Little Italy section of town, which may as well have been the Old Country. "Only it wuzza the football game thatta day, notta the baseball."

The Orioles used to share Memorial Stadium with the Baltimore Colts, before the Colts bolted for a dome in Indiana.

He continued, "The Colts-a hadda terrible day thatta day. Christ, they look-a bad. Anyway, itta wuz inna tha playoffs againsta the Steelers and-a the Steelers wuzza killing the Colts. Something like-a 40 to a-10. And alla the fans-a go home inna the third quarter. They can't standa watcha the Colts-a getta their ass-a kicked anymore. And-a this little plane, like-a something you see flying down-a Ocean City with a sign-a waving-a behind. This fuckin-a plane was a-buzzing around the upper deck all-a day. The whole-a game, buzza buzza," He waved his hand around, imitating a dipping and diving aircraft. "And then, with about a-two or a-three minutes to go, the goddamma thing a-buzzes the stadium again. Buzza buzza. Only this time-a, she don't-a make it. Bam! Right-a into the upper deck, right uppa there." Angelo pointed to the upper deck behind home plate. "I don't-a know how itta happen. But-a the pilot, he don't-a getta hurt. Everybody wuzza OK."

He paused for a second, in wonder. "Course, the police-a beat-a hell outta the guy onna the way to the Northeastern-a District." Nobody doubted Angelo on this count.

"Thank-a God a-the Colts-a wuzza so bad-a that day. Iffa the game-a hadda been any good, those-a people woulda still-a been up there inna those seats." He blessed himself and shook his head. "It woulda been a fuckin' a-disaster you know?"

155

Against the Vikings, we finally boiled over.

I still can't figure the Vikings out. They're silent. I don't think I'd recognize one of them off the field. They're like purple robots. Purple baseball-smashing robots.

Behind 8–3, we needed base runners. Lance coaxed a two-out base on balls from Calvin the home plate umpire.

Calvin is an affable African-American man with a liberal strike zone. He likes to keep the game moving. Sometimes, when the score is lopsided, Calvin will do little tricks to keep himself engaged. Like, instead of his loud, sharp called strike, he'll cut loose a "Whoo-ooop!" Like some kind of screaming bird. The first time I heard it, I thought it was an accident. Maybe Calvin's voice cracked or something. The whole ballpark noticed it, but nobody said anything. The next pitch, another called strike, he did it again.

It was a noise that begged to be repeated. So both benches and many of the players on the field whoo-oooped in unison.

"Hey Calvin, what the hell is that called?" Joe asked from the bench.

"Called keepin' myself int'rested in a boring ballgame," Calvin said.

Tonight, Calvin's partner on the bases is a guy the A's have never seen before. He's short and bookish, a young guy with half-closed eyes behind little glasses. The only other remarkable trait this base umpire possesses is that he doesn't talk.

I don't mean he's soft-spoken. I mean, he doesn't talk at all. When he calls you out, he goes up with the right arm. When you're safe, he bends a little at the waist and flings his arms out. He's even fairly demonstrative about it. But he doesn't make a sound.

After his walk, Lance trotted down to first. Late in the game, it was getting dark and, down five runs, none of us was too focused on the game. Stoffer coached first base. He's the only guy on the team who takes coaching first seriously. When you're a first base coach, your only job is to keep runners like Lance from getting picked off. You don't give signs — they all come from the third base coach. You aren't involved in any strategy. But for Stu, it's a position of authority. Like standing in the first base coach's box means he's actually a coach.

"Back!" Stu yelled, as the pitcher threw to first. The slow-footed Lance wasn't more than three feet off the base. He stepped on first, well ahead of the first baseman's tag. The silent umpire signaled safe.

"They're worried about me," Lance announced to whomever would listen. The first baseman tossed the ball back to the mound. "They know I'm a freakin' racehorse over here. Nice to see somebody in this league respects my speed." Lance's not a fat guy, but he is the owner of a prodigious gut. His big, round belly works hard to push his pants down throughout the game. Thus, Lance's constantly yanking at the top of his pants.

The pitcher threw to first again. "Back!" Stu shouted. Lance got back to the bag, made some more wisecracks. The silent ump signaled that Lance was back in time.

A pitcher could be excused once for keeping Lance Blake close to the base. Once, not twice. The Vikings first baseman ran the ball back to the pitcher, having a brief conference on the mound, their gloves over the mouths so we couldn't read their lips. As if.

The chubby first baseman this time took his position behind Lance. Ahead by five runs, he wisely positioned himself to get an out, rather than worry about a slow base runner. The pitcher stepped on the rubber and Lance took an extra step in his lead.

Suddenly, out of nowhere, the first baseman lunged at Lance, slapping him on the back with his glove. He turned toward the base umpire and produced the ball from his first baseman's mitt, holding it high and trotting across the infield toward the Vikings' third base dugout. The hidden ball trick.

Lance knew immediately what happened. The rest of us didn't. Even the Vikings didn't know. When something happens at one of the bases without a pitch being thrown, nobody can tell what happened. No one's watching the bases. They're watching the pitcher and the batter. The first baseman and pitcher were the only ones in on the trick and they now sat on their bench, laughing their asses off.

And still no word from the base umpire. Even Calvin, the home plate guy, didn't know what the call was. Both teams shouted at the umpires. The A's contended that time had been called and the ball was dead. The Vikings claimed they'd cleverly stolen out number three. But nobody shouted louder than Lance Blake, who had to be restrained from the silent umpire. "You haven't said a word all night!" Lance screamed as Stu moved in from the coaching box. When a baserunner gets into it with an umpire, the base coach's job shifts immediately to saving his teammate from himself, trying to prevent him from doing or saying anything that will get him ejected. Stu wrapped his arms around Lance and tried to pry him away from the ump, who stood silently with his arms folded, eyes still half-closed. "What's the call? You're the umpire! Make a call, you horse's ass!"

Many of the A's took a break from berating the base ump to laugh uncontrollably. Lance had just violated the unwritten code that states you may not call an umpire a name. You may tell him he missed a call. You may tell him he's having a horseshit game and hasn't gotten one right all night. You may not equate him with the ass of a horse. But Lance just did, basically defying the umpire to throw him out of the game. The base umpire turned his back to Lance and said nothing. And just when you believed Lance was as angry as a human being could possibly get, he dug a little deeper. "Don't you turn away from me! I just called you a horse's ass and you don't have the guts to open your mouth and throw me out? What kind of umpire are you?" Lance shrieked, waving his arms around while Stu tried to drag him away.

Calvin came from home plate to his partner's rescue and quieted everyone down. He would get to the bottom of the problem. A hidden ball trick, while technically legal, is a colossally irritating thing to do, especially with a five-run lead. Calvin and the quiet umpire whispered to each other for a few moments. Calvin emerged from the conference, raised his right arm and said, unenthusiastically, "We have an out."

Lance went bananas all over again, this time in Calvin's direction. Lance was clearly wrong. He'd been fooled by a silly trick and he needed to blame anyone but himself. Calvin patiently let Lance wear himself out and Lance politely didn't swear at Calvin or call him a horse's ass. Calvin understood that Lance was angry and didn't want to toss him.

When it was clear he would be allowed to stay in the game, Lance wheeled his wrath toward the A's bench and found Stu. In an instant, Lance's tirade morphed from hilarious to ugly.

"What in the hell were you watching over there? You're supposed to know what they're doing, you stupid jackass! A monkey can coach first! You can't even do that right!"

Every time Stu opened his mouth to defend himself, Lance would shout him back down, each time meaner than the last. The game resumed and Lance continued hammering at Stu.

Lance's nasty tantrums undid any fun we might have been having. And that was the last game Stu played for the A's. He never came back.

Since the loss to the Vikings was on Thursday night, by the time our Saturday morning game against the Hornets rolled around, the A's were still pretty tired and sore. Rod Clement and Kevin were the only pitchers we could use. Abbott and Tim Gaudet both worked four innings on Thursday. Using them on Saturday was out of the question.

Lucky for us, the Hornets barely showed up at all. They started the game with nine players. One more guy showed up in the fourth inning, shirt tail out, no hat, hair all over the place. He turned out to be a kind of metaphor for their whole team that day. The Hornets completely rolled over for us. We handled them, 7–2. I had a couple of hits and got thrown out at the plate. On a close play, I didn't slide. If I had, I most certainly would have been safe.

Now, I'll accept my share of the blame for not sliding. I knew it was going to be a close play. I should have slid. But typically the on-deck batter has a role in all this. When there's a potential play at home plate, the on-deck batter's job is to rush in and get the bat out of the way and tell the runner from third base to slide or cross the plate standing up. When the catcher slap-tagged me on the ass right before my foot hit the plate, the A's bench erupted. "What the hell's the matter with you?" "Christ! You gotta get down!" "Why wouldn't you slide?" I didn't want to sound like a crybaby, but the on-deck batter was nowhere to be seen when I was chugging toward the plate. Then I realized why. The on-deck guy was CJ Demakis, the most oblivious of all the A's.

But the real reason I didn't slide was simple. I was exhausted. Two games in three days and I was completely out of gas. Even in the sweltering heat, that's pathetic.

159

A contributing factor to my exhaustion was the six innings I spent catching. I've been getting some pretty good innings behind the plate lately, sharing the load with Kevin in the hottest part of the season.

There's really nothing quite like catching on a 97-degree day. Good part number one about catching in the heat is, it takes you no time at all to get loose. Every muscle in your body goes slack in this heat and humidity. Good part number two is, I can easily lose 10 pounds on a day like this. Of course, by breakfast the next day, it's all back. But still.

The bad part about catching in this weather is, well, everything else. You didn't know it was possible to sweat like this. Late in the game, on the bench, I took of my catcher's helmet and held it in front of me. A stream of gray sweat poured out of the helmet and splattered on the cement in front of me. I'd soaked in my own brine for so long that my fingertips puckered like I'd been in a bathtub all day.

Today was one of those days when you wonder about human survival. So, let's say it's about this hot every day in various deserts around the globe. But it's dry there. And let's say it's this humid in, say, the Amazon rain forest every day. But it's not this hot. Today, we get the worst elements of two of the cruelest, most stifling climates on the planet. That makes Baltimore, on this particular day, the least pleasant place on earth. I believe that, if Baltimore — or anywhere on earth — was this hot and humid every day, not only would human beings instinctively avoid the place, but the area would be unable to sustain life. Like Venus or Mercury. The only thing that would live in Baltimore would be the heartiest species of mold and fungus.

Obviously, the most important thing to do on days like this is to drink lots of water and Gatorade. And I do. It's common for me, on really hot days, to slug down four quarts or so of Gatorade. I put ice in my catcher's helmet and hold a big ice towel on my head between innings.

But today's game did yield my favorite defensive play: the play at home plate. With a runner at second and two outs, a Hornets batter stroked a single to center field. I knew right away the runner was going to try to score. I popped up from my crouch and kicked the bat out of the baseline, toward the Hornets on-deck circle. Bam Bam Goodrich, our center fielder, charged the bouncing ball and scooped it out of the grass. I stood with a foot on either side of home plate, yelling at Clement to line up as the cutoff man between me and Bam Bam. I stole a glance at the runner rounding third, steaming right at me. The play was going to be close, but I knew we had him.

For me, that's when instinct takes over. Suddenly, catching is part of my DNA. Somewhere along the line, someone told me how to block the plate. But I didn't need to be told. Plate-blocking was written into my code, like breathing.

Clement caught Bam Bam's throw and wheeled on his right foot toward home plate, firing the ball like a laser beam. As soon as he let go of it, I knew Clement's throw was on the money. With the runner coming down the line, the temptation was to peek left at him as he began his slide. But that's the worst thing a catcher can do. It may feel like things are happening in slow motion, but they're not. As soon as you look away from the baseball, you'll never get it back. Or rather, I won't. Not with my eyesight, anyway. I resisted the temptation, instead concentrating on the ball and extending my left leg across home plate, creating a barrier between the runner and a run. Clement's throw drifted a little toward home plate, but not far enough that I had to give up my position. I leaned right a little and watched Clement's throw disappear into my catcher's mitt. I shifted my weight toward the runner, who by now was attempting a hook slide around my giant ham shank of a left leg. Instead, he cut my leg out from under me, propelling me to land on top of him, tagging him while I held the ball securely in the catcher's mitt.

"Show me the ball, catcher!" Mike the umpire yells. Still smothering the ex-baserunner, I removed the ball from my glove and held it high for Mike to see. "He's oooooout!" Mike barks. The guy's foot still hasn't touched the plate. I roll the ball the pitcher's mound for the next pitcher, one of the most satisfying actions a baseball diamond offers.

The A's jog toward the bench from their positions. I get up and tap gloves with Clement, acknowledging his perfect throw. I'm covered in sweat; after rolling around in the dirt at the plate, I look like a big shake 'n' bake.

161

If CJ Demakis wasn't already cemented in infamy, he is now. Today, when somebody mentioned a team party and nobody piped up to volunteer, CJ spoke up reluctantly.

"Well, OK. We can have it at my house."

"Aaaalllrright!"

"Way to go, CJ!"

"Beautiful!"

Then CJ finished his sentence. "If everybody chips in."

"Aaaaawww!"

"Christ! Are you kidding?"

"What a dick!"

The A's thought the wealthiest man in Baltimore should spring for a team party.

Joe said, "CJ, we're all coming to your house and plopping our filthy selves into your immaculate swimming pool. And I'm gonna pee in it."

"Hey! You better not!" CJ protested. "That pool's got a special system in it. You'll mess up the balance! I paid $300,000 for that pool!"

"You'll be lucky if I only pee in it," Joe said.

We lost our next game 9–7 to the Bulls. I played a miserable third base and was amazed that DD still sent me out there. Many of teammates offered me advice on how to field ground balls. I couldn't bear to listen to any of it. I thanked them sarcastically and told them mind their own goddam business.

What's the anatomy of an error?

I take the field between innings, determined not to fail. Which, of course, is different than determined to succeed. Warming up between innings, I'm tentative and choke my throws to first base. I transfer the ball awkwardly from my glove to my bare right hand and pull my arm back too quickly. My throws to first don't have the same zip that they used to.

When the inning starts, I crouch too low, thinking too much about my stance and worrying about the best way to position my feet to move right or left.

Whenever I hear a major leaguer complain about switching positions, I groan. When they use a new defensive position as the reason for their .150 batting average, I always make a wisecrack about what a convenient excuse it is to blame your lousy offense on learning a new defensive position.

But I won't make that wisecrack anymore. Moving from catcher to third base this season has undoubtedly had a profound effect on my hitting. How can that be, since offense and defense are two distinctly different things?

Because — and I wouldn't have believed this before this season — offense and defense are not two distinctly different things. They're two parts of the same thing. When I'm struggling in the field, my confidence sags. And when my confidence sags, my hitting suffers. Necessarily, there's going to be some adjustment to a new position. Every spot on the diamond is different. If you're a first baseman, you can't expect to move to right field without at least a little difficulty. Especially in a league like this one.

When my confidence is shaky in the field, it becomes hard to even imagine making a play in the field. I pick apart the mechanics of a play — making a catch, setting my feet, making a throw — and wonder how anyone ever manages to make even the most routine plays. I know I must've had at least some success at third base this year. I remember making some nice plays. But those plays seem beyond impossible now. Inconceivable.

When you've lost every shred of your confidence, how do you get it back?

For the second time in about a month, I came close to serious injury today. Playing third base with a fast runner at second, I was about even with the bag. Tim Gaudet threw a pitch in the dirt and Kevin struggled a little to come up with it cleanly. Without hesitation, the runner took off in my direction. I hustled to straddle third base and wait for Kevin's throw. One thing the A's gained when Kevin replaced me as catcher was one very strong arm. He was nearly impossible to run on, even with a head start like this baserunner had.

The ball hadn't rolled too far from Kevin. He grabbed it angrily and came up throwing. Kevin took it as a personal affront when anyone dared run on him. Now, even madder than usual, he threw to third with every ounce of strength he could muster. Kevin fired the ball so hard that it appeared out of nowhere. In the instant it took for his throw to travel the 90 feet between us, I marveled at Kevin's arm. While I was marveling, I began my swipe tag at the runner, who was about to arrive half a step later than the ball.

The only trouble was, I started my tag before I caught the ball and the ball hit me flush in the forehead, just above the bill of my hat. I didn't see it, of course. The ball felt like a brick hit me in the head. I was fortunate the ball hit me on the hardest part of the skull, right at the front, where soccer players bop balls with their heads. And like a soccer ball, the baseball flew straight up in the air after it conked me.

I didn't fall over, but I was pretty dizzy. I wasn't sure how many teammates rushed over to make sure I wasn't dead. It looked like a lot, but I was seeing three of everything. Somebody brought some ice from the bench to third base. I removed my hat to apply some ice to my aching head. "Look!" Lance said. "You've got an A on your head!"

"Huh?" I was still pretty groggy and wasn't sure what Lance was saying.

"Your head. Where the ball hit it. There's an A smushed into your head."

I felt the spot and he was right. The ball hit the A's insignia on my hat and left a backwards imprint on my head. And "A" backwards is still "A."

"That's so cool," Abbott said.

Because of early season rainouts, we played the Vikings for the second time in four games. Our 9–6 record, after a 5–0 start to the season, seemed pretty ordinary. We mostly hung around fourth place behind the Giants, Vikings and Bulls. Rainouts had also postponed our game against the Chargers, with whom we were fighting over fourth place. A quick peek at the schedule showed that our last two games of the season were against the Chargers.

In case you're scoring at home, three Athletics — Phil LaSalle, Jack Richmond and Stu Stoffer — have quit the team so far this season. Thus, we're down to 12 guys and we need each of them.

Today's game against the Vikings was a tense affair that we won

12–7. In the fifth inning, I hit a smash to right field for a base hit. The right fielder thought he might have a chance to throw me out at first, the results of a hard hit ball and my slowfootedness. The right fielder snatched the ball on one hop and fired a bullet to first, but I was there in plenty of time. The first baseman tagged me hard anyway, smacking me in the chest with his glove.

It pissed me off that the Vikings thought I was so slow that they could throw me out at first on a legitimate hit. The whole thing was made worse by the hard, high smack tag. If you're going to tag somebody, especially if you don't really have a chance to throw them out, you tag them low. A high tag is just rude. I smacked the first baseman's glove away from me and called time.

Lance, of all people, was coaching first. The Vikings' hidden ball fiasco wasn't far from his mind and he was in no mood for the Rockie first baseman's tricks. As soon as the umpire hollered that time was out, Lance and I simultaneously moved in on the Vikings' first baseman, grabbing his shirt and shaking him as he tried to back away from us. "Listen, you fucking busher, how'd you like me to teach you to play first base?" Lance demanded, with a handful of the first baseman's jersey in both his hands. "Who's slow now, you asshole?," I spat at him, reaching over Lance to grab my own piece of the guy. "You wanna see how fast we kick the shit outta you?"

The Viking first baseman was scrambling backward and stuttering. I imagined Lance and me taking out a whole season's worth of frustrations on this poor shmoe. We both had hold of him, shaking him and pushing him backwards, ready to pound him before his teammates could get to him. I got a look at his face. He was genuinely afraid we were about to beat him up. Lance and I let go of him at the same time and I felt ashamed. I think Lance did too.

After we pounced on their first baseman, the Vikings played a little timid. We literally bullied this win away from a good team.

Kevin Finley probably isn't as strange as I think he is. But in the context of baseball, he's pretty damn odd.

"You guys ever see Kate Kavern?" Finley sat in the middle of bench, looking away from the batter's box.

"No," O'Hare said, his elbows resting on his catcher's leg guards. "Who's Kate Kavern?"

"Oh my god, dude, you're so missing out," Finley said, longingly. He said it the way some people talk about Paris in May or the greatest meal they've ever eaten.

Now I was curious. "Why? Who is she?" I asked.

Finley slid over on the bench to get closer to O'Hare and me. "She's this adult film star that we really like a lot," he whispered.

"Hmm-mm," O'Hare said, nodding his head slowly. "And by 'we,' ...?"

"My wife and me," Finley said.

"Your wife. I see." O'Hare glanced at me like he'd struck gold.

"Yeah, dude. We're going to meet her soon. She's gonna be in Delaware and my wife's gonna get her for us for my birthday."

"Uh huh. And, when you say 'get her for us' ...." O'Hare stopped himself, holding in a laugh.

"We're all gonna get it on, dude," Finley growled. "All three of us. My wife likes girls, too."

"Girls too! Hey, that's great!" O'Hare said. "Really. It's important to be able to share in a relationship."

"Dude, you're damn right." Finley was a million miles away, engrossed in carnal fantasy in the bottom of the fourth inning.

Finley is a dude, in the strictest sense. He's got a buzz cut, wears expensive shades and has what you can tell is a huge — I mean huge — tattoo peeking out from the back of his jersey. If the top of it is any indication, the tattoo covers his whole back.

"So, lemme ask you, Kevin, is this thing going to take place in Delaware for, say, legal reasons?" I asked.

"Huh?"

"I mean, do you have to go to Delaware to get it on with... Ms. Kavern, is it? ... to get it on with Ms. Kavern because of some kind of law here in Maryland?"

"No, no. She's gonna be doing a show up there."

"A show, huh?"

O'Hare was fascinated. "And will there be any sort of— what's the word I'm looking for — remuneration for this transaction?"

"Any what?"

"Any money. Will any money change hands? Do you have pay Kate Kavern to get it on with you and your wife."

"Well, yeah," Finley said, annoyed. "I mean, she don't work for free."

Finley, or Caligula, as he came to be known after revealing his debauch, never talked much to us again. I can't say I blame him. Hey, it's no business of ours who he and his wife go to bed with. He was just trying to share with his teammates. But baseball, more than any other sport, abhors non-conformity. If you're different, you're a flake or a weirdo.

In many ways, I've felt out of place in baseball. For some reason, more than other sports, baseball attracts political conservatives. I don't know why, but every team I've ever played on has resembled a John Birch Society meeting. And, like a lot of conservatives, ballplayers are goons. If you're different in any way, they don't let you forget it.

I was different in high school. I'm different now. I embrace individuality and creativity. I'm typically the one on the team who gets a pile of shit for my liberal politics. And I act like I don't care, but the boneheads are relentless. There's no end to the joy they get from hounding me. But when Finley confided in O'Hare and me about a sleazy three-way with a high-end hooker, I was privately glad to join the crowd and call him a weirdo. Now he's Caligula.

Before Washington, D.C., had its own team, the Baltimore Orioles were the capital city's team by default. George Will and Larry King were always at the stadium. You could predict which politicians and operatives would be at the park, depending on who was in town. Pat Leahy, Ted Kennedy and the New England delegation would pack the park for the Red Sox series. When foreign dignitaries visited the White House during the summer months, you could be sure that whomever was president at the time would bring them to an O's game. Just like if you had out of town guests for a few days: "What the hell are we going to do with your brother for three days?" "Let's take him to a ballgame."

During George Bush the elder's administration, the White House and the State Department hosted an important state visit from the president of Egypt. Naturally, having nothing else to do at night, Bush brought him to the Orioles-Minnesota Twins game on a Tuesday night. And just like you'd do if it was your kid's birthday, somebody in the White House called ahead and told the Orioles front office that the president of Egypt would be at the game and, y'know, it'd be nice if you could announce his name and everything. Maybe put it up on the scoreboard.

Today, in the heightened age of security, when the president is in the ballpark, every fan gets patted down and snipers perch atop the stadium, scopes trained on the crowd. And while it wasn't always this bad, you always could guess when the president was at the game. Lots of hustle, lots of strange guys in suits. A buzz in the air.

So at the O's-Twins game, before the national anthem but after PA announcer Rex Barney thanked the evening's Milk Duds Honorary Bat Boy and Girl, he made a special announcement. And as always, Barney paused every few syllables to let his voice echo out of the stadium.

"Ladies and gentlemen.
Your attention please.
Joining us this evening
are two special guests.
The President
of the United States
George Bush (extra long pause for applause)
and the President
of Egypt
Hosni...
Mubarek.
An Orioles welcome
to our guests.
Thank yooooou."

Just like that. Like he was introducing Duffy Dyer or T-Bone Shelby. You haven't lived until you've heard Hosni Mubarek's name announced over the PA system at a ballgame. Baseball is the great equalizer.

168

Remember when the Pope came to Camden Yards? They covered up all the Budweiser and Marlboro ads and the Pontiff said mass. I wasn't there, but I saw pictures. It looked like a cross between a ballgame and a concert. Is it the Pope or the Steve Miller Band? He was in the middle of the field, as though he was presiding over an enormous pep rally.

It just struck me funny that the Pope said the highest of high masses at the ballpark in my city. I half expected Rex Barney to announce,

"Ladies and gentlemen,
your attention please.
Direct your attention
to the area behind second base,
where, for your spiritual enrichment,
the holy Eucharist
will be administered
by Pope John Paul
(pause)
The Second.
Thank yooooooooou."

169

Thirteen

Baseball uniforms aren't really meant to be comfortable, I guess. Or anyway, they're not comfortable on me. I'm not the kind of guy who wears clothes easily, if you know what I mean. A jacket or a pair of pants off the rack fits me different than most men. Which is to say, poorly. I have an XXL waist and M arms and legs.

I found a pair of baseball pants a few years ago that fit perfectly. They were exactly the right length and the waist was perfect: stretchy but firm enough to stay up. But the company that made my favorite pants went out of business soon after I bought my pair.

The pants were white when I bought them. But after two or three seasons of infield dirt and streaming sweat — not to mention my haphazard hot water washing technique of throwing the whole sweaty bright green, gold and white mess into the washer together, resulted in a new color entirely.

The weird color didn't bother me. I wore the pants for every game we played, knowing their days were numbered. Sadly, the treasured trousers finally succumbed after a third base slide and I was forced to hunt for a new pair. Nobody made pants like those anymore. Every pair I tried was wrong. Too cheap. Too tight. Too long. Too loose. Nothing's worse than a pair of pants that don't fit right. To this day, I search for the right pair of baseball pants. I switch between two or three pairs, none of them just right.

Players in the Over-30 League are no different than Little Leaguers or high school players. We see the trends in the way big leaguers wear their uniforms and copy them as quickly as we can. It takes no time at all for fashion trends to find their way from baseball's cathedrals to dusty sandlots.

For example, only players wishing to call attention to themselves wear the cuffs of their pants high anymore. Today's players wear them, if not bunched on top of their shoes, certainly low enough so that only a discreet sock peeks out.

And socks are another statement. Gone are the days of stirrups and sanitary socks, the thin, white cotton socks that players wore between their feet and their stirrups. Today, players wear only solids, which makes sense, really. They're just socks. What possible purpose could stirrup socks serve? I've never known.

When I joined the A's, they asked me what number I wanted to wear. I told them I wanted the number nine. There are all sorts of reasons why nine is the perfect baseball number. Nine innings. Nine players on defense. Nine is also a holy number somewhere, three plus three plus three. Nine is a great catcher's number, having to do with strength and energy. I don't know. It just seems like you should have a good reason for picking your number.

For the first time all year, we played the Chargers. For the past three seasons, the Chargers have looked a lot like the Kings. By which I mean, terrible. They had one guy who could play and 14 who really couldn't. But this year, with two games remaining on the regular season schedule, the A's and the Chargers have the same record.

We piled on the Chargers like an avalanche. For the first time since I joined the league, the A's beat an opponent using the Slaughter Rule. The Slaughter Rule says that if, after four innings, a team leads an opponent by at least 10 runs, the game's over. We only played four innings against the Chargers and it felt like the game took all day. The final score was 17–1. If we'd kept playing, it might have been 80–1. They just couldn't get us out. "What's the big deal about the Chargers?," one of our guys asked. "I thought they were supposed to be good."

In the next game, we found out what the big deal about the Chargers was. They could play. I have no idea how they could stink so bad one game and play so well the next. But they did. The Chargers beat us 3–2 in the last regular season game.

So, the Athletics finished the regular season with 11 wins and seven losses. That's a fine season, but after a red-hot start, we're a little disappointed. We have no right to be, though. This is the first season we've even finished with a winning record. We're not the best team in the league. We lost our share of games that we should have won. But we're not the worst team in the league either. The Bulls are the only team that really seemed to have our number, beating us twice, 9–7 and 8–5.

FINAL REGULAR SEASON STANDINGS

Team	Wins	Losses	Ties	PCT.
GIANTS	14	3	1	.778
VIKINGS	13	4	1	.722
BULLS	12	6	0	.667
ATHLETICS	**11**	**7**	**0**	**.611**
CHARGERS	11	7	0	.611
PILOTS	9	9	0	.500
HORNETS	6	12	0	.333
TIGERS	5	13	0	.278
KINGS	4	14	0	.222
BROWNS	4	14	0	.222

The top eight teams go to the postseason tournament. We finished fourth in the regular season. So, in the first round, we draw the Chargers, with whom we share an identical record.

The postseason tournament is double elimination. Lose twice and you're out. It's a pretty grueling affair, really. Two or three games a week in the hottest part of the year is almost enough to make you hope for a quick exit from the tournament.

Which has been very much the A's style since I've been in the league. We might win one or two in the tournament. Make a little noise against the eventual champions, even. But we're usually done after three or four games. And really, nobody's too disappointed. We've never thought of ourselves as a championship team.

True to form, at no time this year did I fool myself into thinking the Athletics were good enough to win the championship. In the hottest of hot streaks, I knew one fundamental thing about our team. We might be talented. We might be determined. And we might be bullies. But we don't know how to really slam the door. When the playoffs come around, I told myself all year, we'll fold right up.

Well, we didn't fold up. We pounded the Chargers in the first game, scoring six runs in the first inning and never looking back. We lost a close one to the Giants.

We beat the Tigers. We finally beat the Bulls when it counted.

Which set up a showdown with the Giants, who haven't lost a playoff game yet. They beat the Kings, they beat us, they beat the Pilots.

What's all this mean? It means the A's are in the championship series. Since the Giants haven't lost yet, we're going to have to beat them twice. Since they already beat us once, in the second round, they only have to beat us once to win their third straight league title.

After the 1988 season, I had no intention of returning to the Orioles grounds crew. I'd had a great experience, even as awful as the season was. But I wasn't sure I wanted to commit to 81 games and a team buried in last place from April to September. If you actually root for a team, you can really only watch them lose so many times.

Also, the dynamic of a day at the ballpark changes when you're not allowed to leave. Coming to the park and watching baseball games became work during my season on the grounds crew. It was a job I liked, but still, it was a job. My favorite team was my employer and I owed them something more than buying a ticket. Fans regularly leave in the seventh inning of one-sided or uninteresting games. But when you work for the team, you can't pick up and leave. You're there for every pitch of every inning.

Anyway, I was supposed to be in school. Like a noisy muffler tied on with a coat hanger, my grades bounced and dangled precariously, scraping the road and spraying sparks, threatening to let go at any moment. And it was impossible for me to get any school work done at the stadium. I'd bring my books to the ballpark and then play hundred-inning Wiffleball games in the bullpen.

I spent so many hours at the ballpark during the season that huge chunks of my college semester just whizzed by. One of my literature professors commented that, if you didn't have an Orioles schedule, you could tell whether the team was in town by looking at my quiz scores in his class. A decent passing score meant two things. One, the Birds were out of town and two, I'd had time to at least skim the book.

Given my academic woes, I was perpetually on the verge of getting tossed out of school. I lived my life one "D" away from academic suspension. Thus, throughout high school and college, summer wasn't summer without summer school. History classes, math classes, science classes. If I wasn't repeating some flunked class from the previous term, I was playing catch up, trying to earn enough credits to graduate in a reasonable number of years.

I learned the hard way in 1988 that summer classes and a big league grounds crew job were not compatible. Essays went unwritten, books went uncarefully read or not read at all.

As the 1989 Orioles season got underway, my college grades resembled that old black and white film clip of the guy trying to fly some kind of winged contraption just before the whole thing collapses onto itself. I'd gotten letters from the university, I'd had meetings with people in the administration building, informing me that I was a breath away from getting bounced right out of school.

I also hadn't done myself any favors by getting arrested in April for a ridiculous drunken prank involving the theft of a big plastic sign that welcomed visitors to the university. After a 25-cent beer night at some awful sticky-floored college bar where my roommate and I had left behind about 10 bucks apiece, we walked home and thought it would be the funniest thing in the world to put that sign in our little off-campus house. The administration didn't get the joke and put the screws to my roommate and me. Our status was, as the university's attorneys put it, "endangered."

I didn't reapply for my grounds crew job and the '89 season at Memorial Stadium got underway without me. Both the season and the academic semester unfolded with promise. The Orioles caught fire in May and June, at one point winning 13 of 14. My grades weren't quite as hot as the O's, but they could reasonably be described as over .500.

As I barreled into my summer classes, the Birds went on another tear and I couldn't stand it any longer. During a day game in the middle of June, I visited the grounds crew and asked the Tarp Nazi for my job back.

Just like that, I was back in uniform, suddenly a senior member of the crew, offered much more respect than during my rookie season. I could have bullpen duty whenever I wanted it. I rarely did the infield drag. A time or two, I even directed the crew as it rolled the tarp back onto its big metal tube. Santarone no longer yelled at me and the Tarp Nazi was even pleasant.

I was rolling through a British literature course and a literary research and criticism class. Early grades were strong and, if I could prove to the administration that my little prank with the sign was just college-kid wackiness, I was on target for a fall graduation. My summer grades and the Orioles were both flying high.

After a five-game win streak in July, the Orioles sat atop the American League East, seven and a half games ahead of the Yankees, eight and a half ahead of Toronto. But a 14-game road trip nearly derailed the season. The O's lost four in Oakland, three in Minnesota, three in Kansas City and the first three in Boston. That's 13 straight, if you're counting. At the end of the swoon, a dropped doubleheader at Fenway, Baltimore clung to a one-game lead over the Red Sox, with the Brewers, Jays, Tigers and Yanks all close behind. And right along with the Orioles, I went on a cold streak of my own. Engrossed with the Orioles' chase for the division title, I botched a couple quizzes, left one or two books unread and the momentum shifted. Graduation — or even avoiding suspension — was no longer a lock.

The rest of the season and the rest of my summer semester were a horse race. Like the Orioles, I spent July and the first weeks of August recovering from a plummeting spiral. The O's recovered for a time. But after a lopsided August loss in Cleveland, they finally coughed up their division lead.

Summer school ended and I came up short. Even before the letter arrived, I knew I was done. I walked around nonchalant, like a basketball player after he's fouled out. Everybody knows you're out of the game. Just go sit down, already. At last, a letter came in the mail refunding my fall registration and banishing me for a semester. I could petition the university to let me back in to finish my degree, but not until I'd sat one out.

It could have been worse, I figured. They could have made me wait a whole year, or even not let me back in at all. A one-semester suspension was pretty reasonable, especially considering the felony charges the humorless administration was filing against my roommate and me.

That year, the O's got so close to the playoffs that there was talk of the grounds crew splitting one of the postseason bonuses the players got. When you're broke, the prospect of a few thousand unexpected bucks is pretty exciting. During games, guys on the grounds crew sat around and divvied up imaginary money. We had a new, even more compelling reason to root, root, root for the home team.

But on the last weekend of the season, Toronto edged out the Orioles for the 1989 division title. For years, baseball people talked about the Orioles' near-miracle finish. One of the worst teams in the history of big league baseball somehow recovered the very next season and stayed alive for 160 games.

And, true to their word, the university finally did let me back in and I finished college without incident.

Game 1 of the A's-Giants playoff showdown was on a weeknight, after most guys got off work. There were thunderstorms passing through Baltimore and the sky threatened all day.

After infield practice, DD read the lineup. My name wasn't in it. No wonder, really. I wasn't hitting much and I was a mess at third base.

Naturally, George Bloch started for the Giants. Tim Gaudet led off the game for us with a single. Then, with two outs, Rod Clement hit a towering triple in the gap in left center. Tim scored easily. Kevin popped up to end the inning.

In the bottom of the inning, Gaudet gave up three runs, including a two-run homer by Bloch. DD had decided to start Gaudet and then bring Abbott in to finish things up. Assuming Scott was effective, it would give us a chance to make a comeback if we needed to.

We needed to.

The ball would have been 15 feet over the fence — had there been a fence. Soccer season had taken over and the county rec and parks department took down the baseball fence in the middle of the playoffs. Turns out, that might have won my team a championship.

George Bloch launched a Tim Gaudet fastball high and deep into the early-evening sky. The ball sailed to straight-away center, where Abbott was stationed until he took over the late innings from Tim. From third base, I could barely see Abbott, his back to the infield, in a full sprint. With late summer storms hovering around, the sky turned a silvery gray, like a mood ring. Abbott got a perfect jump on the ball. With the fence gone, Abbott sprinted unafraid after the ball, the lower half of his body disappearing down a slight hill. He was well into no-man's land, but the umpires had said before the game that balls beyond the phantom fence were in play until they landed in the little stream beyond left field.

Figuring the batter was good for at least a triple, I covered my base, straddling third and getting ready to line up a cutoff man.

But the ball kept sailing and Abbott kept running. Somehow, he had a play.

The ball vanished into Scott's glove and he vanished down the hill. He returned the ball like a laser beam to the infield. Abbott had made the play of the year in the biggest game of the year.

The catch energized the A's in a way I'd never seen. Tim found a groove and flatly refused to let runners on base. In the fourth, down 3 to 1, Lance reached on an error. Then something truly crazy happened. Lance stole second.

You know that story of the elderly woman who suddenly summons the strength to lift an automobile to rescue her trapped baby grandson? That's kind of how Lance stole second base. He ran like his pants were on fire. When he arrived well ahead of the ball, he slid hard. "Safe!" the base umpire boomed. Lance struggled to his feet and brushed off his uniform. He looked at the bench and pumped his fist. Eleven screaming A's and their fans climbed all over one another. We were no longer kidding around. Clement singled to right field and Lance scored, huffing and puffing. 3–2. Clement stole second and scored on Abbott's base hit. 3–3.

In the top of the sixth, with two outs, Giants reliever Carl Leisler struck out Tim. But the catcher missed the third strike and the ball caromed off the backstop and he missed it again. Tim shot down the line ahead of the throw. With a gentle rain falling, Lance drove a single to right field. Tim rounded second, determined to make third base. Giants right fielder Rich Cantoni played the ball perfectly on the run and came up throwing. Tim looked dead. Except the wet baseball slipped out of Cantoni's hand while he was throwing it. The ball sailed high over the Giants third baseman, allowing Tim to score. 4–3, A's.

In the bottom of the sixth, the Giants' number six hitter Don Jackson tagged a leadoff double off Abbott. The next batter popped to shallow center field. With one out and a runner at second base in a one-run game, Cantoni hit a long fly ball to center field. Bam Bam Goodrich drifted back, back, back still facing the infield. The ball kept flying and it became clear that Bam Bam had misjudged the ball. He turned around suddenly, sprinting toward the outfield, straining to keep track of the ball. On a dead run, Bam Bam reached out and made the catch. He jogged to a stop and held the ball high, like a fisherman showing off a king mackerel, his back to the infield.

Bam Bam had no idea how many outs there were.

Jackson wisely tagged at second and charged toward third. The A's screamed like they were drowning.

"Throw it in! Throw it in!"

"Bam Bam! That's only two outs!"

"Aaaaaa!"

Bam Bam heard the din and recovered from his bizarre lapse. He threw the ball like a balloon toward Clement, who'd set up as a cutoff man in short left. Jackson was now rounding third and planning to tie the game.

Clement took Bam Bam's throw, spun and threw a bullet to O'Hare on one bounce. Play at the plate.

Jackson's sweeping hook slide wasn't quite enough. He was out by an inch. A perfect throw from Clement and a perfect tag by O'Hare bailed Bam Bam out of what would have been, as they say, a costly blunder.

When he reached the bench, Bam Bam swore he was decoying the runner into trying to take the extra base. "That's exactly the way I planned it," he grinned.

We got another break in the top of the seventh. After we put a couple runners on base, the rain began to fall harder. A lot harder. The umpires waited as long as they could before ending a championship game. But when an enormous, white lightning bolt hit beyond right field, followed by an immediate violent thunder crack, the home plate ump yelled, "That's game!" and ran off the field. The A's, unafraid of lightning striking again, celebrated in the driving rain and mud.

In the post-season double elimination tournament, the Giants and the A's were all even. The exhausting game left us one win from the championship.

I didn't do much in the game. I got a base hit that didn't amount to much. Fielded a couple of grounders at third. Tagged a runner out. Once I got in the game, I concentrated on not making errors. Which is a little less satisfying than envisioning yourself a game-saving hero.

Fourteen

Today, a few hundred miles separate my dad and me. We don't see each other very often. He and my mother are the busiest people I know. Trying new things, traveling, fussing over my sister's kids.

Baseball doesn't mean as much to Dad as it used to. The huge salaries and the endless hype have distanced him from the game. He still watches, still goes to a minor league game now and then. He reads the box scores. And his memories and stories of baseball are endless. Last time we were together he told a story I'd never heard before. My parents traveled to New York on their honeymoon in the winter of 1966. They went to some fancy midtown nightclub and ran into Pirate infielder Dick Groat, who happened to be there with his wife. My father, who's never once missed a chance to introduce himself to whomever he likes, struck up a conversation with Groat. Dad told the shortstop that he and my mom were fresh newlyweds and Pirate fans from Altoona. They all talked and laughed and danced at the nightclub. They returned to their tables at opposite ends of the room for dinner and some show or other. And, near the end of the evening, the Groats sent my parents a bottle of champagne, with a note of congratulations attached. My dad misses days when ballplayers were a little more human, a little more likely to wind up in the same nightclub as you and do something nice. I tell him there are still guys like that. But his mind's pretty much made up.

Anymore, he's a college sports guy through and through. And since basketball and football are the dominant college sports, they're what he's into. I think college football is terrifically entertaining. And college basketball is even better, if you ask me. But, the same way my father laments big league baseball's spiral into the depths of greed, I

181

hold my nose when I watch "student athletes" playing football. Every day, it seems, some college basketball or football player — or worse, a coach — winds up under the "Juridprudence" heading in the newspaper. The charade of trotting these kids onto the field or court and pretending it has anything to do with college seems silly. Why not just pay them and lose the phony connection with higher education? And my dad knows this, just like I know that baseball is run by greedy owners and an out-of-control player's union.

So, over the years, my dad and I have negotiated an unspoken compromise. I follow college sports just enough to have something to talk about with my father. And he follows big league baseball just enough to talk with me.

We talk on the phone often. He mails me little news clippings from the sports page of his hometown paper. He goes to booster club meetings and gets autographs, asking coaches to sign them "to Patrick." Sometimes, when my dad and I are together, I long to talk about more than just sports. But most times, I don't. I'm grateful for the gift.

A couple years ago, my father went to a remote city in China on a business trip. He's always been a frequent domestic business traveler. But China was a record for him.

The trip was brutal. Twenty-something hours, three plane changes, god-knows-how-many miles. Then, when he got there, two weeks of intense work. And twenty-some more hours home.

Naturally, he brought back gifts for everyone. He brought my mother a beautiful set of Chinese candles. He brought my sister a Chinese silk scarf. Deb got a hand-painted Chinese tea set.

He brought me a left-handed batter.

China is known for a lot of things. But baseball is not among them. They play other games, do other things. Yes, there are Asian countries where baseball is popular. But not China.

Nevertheless, at some crowded street bazaar in Fujiu, China, he spotted a two-foot, frosted glass statue of a left-handed batter, crouched in an odd batting stance. The statue sits on a heavy marble base and the batter holds a brass baseball bat. The whole thing probably weighs 30 pounds. He had it wrapped up and brought it home.

It's not remarkable that my father bought me a less than beautiful statue of a ballplayer. What's remarkable is that he lugged it all the way around the world to give to me.

The championship game was played late on Sunday afternoon. For the second game in a row, the Giants scored all of their runs in the first inning. It always seemed to take the Athletics a little while before we started concentrating. Tim gave up two runs and DD lifted him for Clement. By the time the first inning was over, the Giants had four runs. They were the last four runs of their season.

Carl Leisler started on the mound for the Giants. Leisler is 51 and in terrific shape. He's incredibly vain and dyes his thick hair blonde. Like Bloch, he changes speeds and can be tough to hit. Still, he's definitely their number two pitcher. He's good, but he's not Bloch.

Leisler was a reliever in the last game and he struck me out looking. That's maybe the second time all year I've struck out looking. I'm a free swinger. I'm not in this league to draw walks. Anyway, in my first at-bat, in the third inning, I fought Leisler hard. He got ahead of me at one ball and two strikes, but I raked a single to right field and scored our first run of the game on a clutch hit from Chris Nichols.

That's all we got in the third. We added one in the fourth to make the score 4–2 Giants. They borrowed our strategy of using their ace over the last four innings and brought in Bloch after Leisler. Turns out, Bloch can pitch in relief too.

Bloch was unhittable. Worse, the farther along he went, the more we started believing he was unhittable. We swallowed every bait he threw us. We struck out, we grounded out, we popped up. No one hit a ball hard for almost four innings. He mowed down the first 11 Athletics he faced.

In fact, we were down to our very last out of the season before any of us got on base. Joe banged a solid two-out single up the middle. Alex hit a hard ground ball right to the second baseman... who fielded the ball cleanly and threw it right over the first baseman's head. The ball rolled all the way to the batting cage, automatically allowing the runners to advance an extra base. Down 4 to 2, the A's had men at second and third with two outs. Demakis at the plate.

I'm on deck.

I was pretty sure Bloch was going to pitch to Demakis, even with first base open. He'd rather face a right-handed batter than a lefthander like me. For most of the years we've played together, CJ Demakis hasn't been a very good hitter. He's impatient, especially with runners on base, and he's got no power at all. On the other hand, I'm a guy who can hit... just not this year.

I realized in the on-deck circle, with our whole season on the line, that I've rarely had any rhythm this season. Maybe it was the position change. Maybe it was the drama that swirled around the team all year. Maybe I just wasn't very good.

I tapped dirt out of my cleats, messed with my batting gloves, swung a bat with a weighted donut on it.

Since CJ wasn't very patient, he was likely the last out of the season. If he did get a hit, it probably wouldn't go far enough to score both runs and I'd still get an at-bat.

I pretended I was my own therapist and asked myself how I felt about that. Would I want to be the guy at the plate in this situation? Players always say they do, but I believe many of them secretly wish the opportunity would pass them by. Do I need that kind of pressure in my life? But saving our team in the championship would immediately erase from history the errors, the pop-ups, the dinks to the first baseman. It would make the whole year a success, both for me and for my team.

As I debated with myself whether or not I wanted to be at the plate, Bloch's first pitch to Demakis hit him squarely in the back. The ultimate control pitcher, Bloch drilled a right-handed banjo hitter to load the bases. For me.

I stood motionless, hyperventilating a little. Can you hyperventilate a little? One last practice swing. Walking slowly toward the plate, I heard the ballpark buzzing. Some of that was the tense hum of the situation and some of it was my ears ringing. I held my bat by the barrel end and tapped the handle on the ground. The weighted donut slid to the grass.

"Let's go now, Pat."

"You da man, Smitty."

"Right man, right spot. You're the guy we want up there."

The A's encouraged me quietly. The Giants had a meeting on the pitcher's mound. This really can't be happening, can it? Has it all come to this? It has. A base hit will tie the game.

This is exactly why I play baseball, isn't it? For these opportunities? This really is a once-in-a-career chance, a shot at redeeming a tough season. A chance to come through for your teammates. A chance to be the hero.

I looked down at DD coaching third base before I stepped into the box. He clapped his hands and gave the me the "Go get 'em" sign.

I'd already made up my mind I was going to take a strike. With the bases loaded, I owed it to my team to try to get a run home any way I could. Plus, it's better to make the pitcher work and try to get a favorable count. Then you can look for your pitch.

I stepped in and called time, holding my left palm up to the umpire and digging a little hole in the batter's box with the front of my left shoe. I settled and waited, with no intention of swinging, no matter how fat the pitch was. Bloch kicked his leg high and threw a fastball right down the middle. Strike one.

I stepped out and took a couple practice swings. Damn. He must've known I wasn't going to swing. How'd he know that? Bloch knew how to stay out of a hole. He challenged me with a fastball at the knees and got himself ahead in the count. Immediately, he's on the attack and I'm on the defensive.

I dug back into the box and settled into a little rhythm, wobbling my bat slowly over my head.

With no fear whatsoever, Bloch threw another fastball, this time up and in. He understood that, with a two-run lead, even if his high and tight fastball gets away from him and either hits me or gets past the catcher, he'll still have a one-run lead. Instinct made me bend backwards away from the plate to avoid getting hit in the head. One ball, one strike.

Earlier in the year, you'll recall, I got a hit off Bloch with two strikes. How? By taking whatever he gave me. Don't try to do too much with a George Bloch pitch. That time, he threw me a change-up outside and I poked it over the shortstop's head and it faded down the left field line.

Just like last time, Bloch's next pitch was off-speed, low and away. But this time I took the bait. Rather than move with the pitch, I swung too hard and tried to pull the ball to right, visions of game-tying RBIs in my head. But I was way out in front of the pitch. I shifted all my weight to my front foot too early and the instant the bat hit the ball, I knew the A's were done. I tapped a dribbling ground ball right back to Bloch, who picked it up and threw it like a dart to first. As I ran desperately down the line, praying for a miracle error, I saw the first baseman catch Bloch's throw with his foot against the bag. Then I saw him fling his glove and the ball high into the air, springing toward the middle of the infield, arms raised over his head.

I crossed first base way too late, stopped running and dropped to the ground. On one knee, I slumped about five yards behind first base. My throat tightened up and my eyes stung. I shut them as tight as I could. I wanted to cry. I wanted to fight. I wanted to stay in this spot for the rest of my life. I felt angry, embarrassed, heartbroken and suddenly sick to my stomach. There wasn't a strong enough swear word to express bouncing back to the pitcher to end our shot at the league title. I couldn't throw a helmet far enough or kick the grass hard enough. So I just stayed like that for a little while. I stood and looked at the A's forming a line in the infield, shaking hands with their rivals. I joined the line.

I guess I shook hands with all the Giants. I don't really remember.

The whole thing was over. The inning, the game, the season. The end. So long. See ya next year.

One at-bat. After six months, the whole season came down to one at-bat. If I got a hit, it was a great year. If I didn't, the season's a bust. And I didn't get a hit.

Is there a worse, more impotent way to make an out than by bouncing back to the pitcher? I guess I could have struck out. That might have been worse. What if I'd hit a shot and gotten robbed by the defense? Would that have felt any better? In the end, an out's an out, I suppose.

As soon as the handshakes were out of the way, the A's scattered. A couple of them hung around, but mostly guys just said their brief goodbyes and drove off. I had a cooler full of beer and a box of cigars.

But they were for winners. Most guys on the team were gone before DD could even call a team meeting.

Which was just as well, really. When the season's over, the A's aren't really a team anymore. We don't get together off the field. Some of us have tried and the gatherings have been pleasant enough. Christmas parties, football games, happy hours. But really, the only thing the A's have in common with one another is baseball.

So those of us who did stick around for awhile after the game — Chris, Rod, Joe, Abbott, Kevin, me — were no longer a baseball team. Just a handful of guys drinking beer and wearing smelly uniforms that happened to match.

Fifteen

Any time a player in the Over-30 League complains about rules or umpires or his teammates — complains about anything, really — someone will invariably tell him to "go play Ponce."

For years, I had no idea what that meant. I figured it was some cryptic way to tell a complainer to go to hell. But at some point this year, I figured it out. When someone says "go play Ponce," it means, roughly, "if you don't like it, go play in the Ponce de Leon League."

The Washington, D.C., suburbs of Maryland and Virginia have their own baseball league for older guys who still want to play. It's called the "Ponce de Leon League," named for the 15th-century Spanish explorer famous for his pursuit of the fountain of youth. The Ponce League, as everyone calls it, is far more regulated than our league. There's a rule for everything in Ponce. For example, their teams have rotating batting orders, meaning if you were on deck when your team made the last out, you lead off the next game. That kind of thing.

The Ponce League bills itself as "competitive, but not too competitive." And they have rules to keep you from getting out of line.

There are no league standings. Their brochure says something like, "hey, guys have enough competition in their day to day lives. Who needs competition on the baseball diamond?" The league also has a thing about guys who take the whole thing too seriously. They make a grand claim to have no assholes in their league. That's simply not possible. Baseball, great as it is, is loaded with jerks.

And you have to learn to make your own way when the jerks start taking up too much room. Maybe you have to find your own inner jerk. Or maybe you have to make some heroic stand to reclaim the game from the creeps.

189

Taking wins and losses from the game, never having a true leadoff hitter or cleanup hitter, scouring the league of guys who are too competitive: the sanitization and democratization of baseball. Not a terrible idea, I guess. But all those rules strike me as an attempt to regulate out of baseball one of its most precious assets: disappointment.

Baseball is, far more often than not, a spectacular, perfect disappointment. It's been noted many times that a batter who is successful about three times out of ten is on his way to Cooperstown.

But that batter is also unsuccessful — thus, disappointed — about 70 percent of the time. Baseball is one disappointment after another, making small successes feel that much better and making large successes feel otherworldly. It's like the guy who hits himself over the head with a hammer because it feels so good when he stops.

Your favorite big league team plays enough games in one season that you can experience one or two of those monumental triumphs each year, no matter how bad the team is. On the field, in the stands, at home on your couch. Your summer may be filled with disappointments, but it only takes one of those moments where you raise your arms over your head and yell as loud as you can to make it worth all the headache. You can't win 'em all. But nor, in baseball, can you lose 'em all.

Disappointment is the glue that holds the game together. At every level I've encountered baseball, both as a player and as a fan, the game has been one long disappointment, interrupted by periodic bursts of ecstasy.

In 1996, 13 years removed from their last sniff of the postseason, the Baltimore Orioles were second-best in the recently realigned American League East. And that was good enough for a playoff spot. The first post season game in Baltimore since 1983 and the first ever at Camden Yards would be a weekday afternoon game against the big slugging Cleveland Indians.

My friend Mahoney and I had the worst seats in the ballpark that day. It's been said that Oriole Park at Camden Yards has no bad seats. But we got the closest thing to them. And I had more fun at that ballgame than at any other game I ever attended. Oriole centerfielder Brady Anderson launched a leadoff homer to put the O's up 1–0 in the bottom of the first. The Indians' Manny Ramirez tagged returned the favor in the top of the second to tie the game at one. But in the bottom of the second, fan favorite left fielder B.J. Surhoff hit a one-out solo homer of his own and the Birds wouldn't trail again. Baltimore's rent-a-slugger Bobby Bonilla added a grand slam in the sixth and, for a few moments, I thought the left field upper deck at Camden Yards might just collapse under all the dancing and jumping up and down.

The game turned into a huge party. Every time the Orioles pushed across another run, the stadium rocked a little harder. It was one of those days that felt like a dream that you didn't want to end. No matter how many beers I bought, I never ran out of money.

It wasn't a great time in my life. I was out of work. We had money problems. I even had the flu. But for three and a half hours, I experienced only joy. The O's won 10–4 and it remains the most fun I've ever had at a ballgame. That afternoon was an exorcism of all the lousy years, all the failed prospects, all the one-run losses and all the thumpings the Orioles endured at the hands of the Blue Jays, Red Sox and Yankees. The game pressed the reset button on my fandom.

That afternoon game against Cleveland couldn't have meant as much as it did if Orioles fans hadn't suffered through so many disappointments. You gotta be lost if you're gonna be saved.

The Ponce de Leon League has taken the heartbreak out of the game. And, proportionately, they've stripped the game of its thrill. It's got to mean something when you hit into a double play. Otherwise, it doesn't mean anything when you hit a bases-clearing double. And that would be tragic.

Ponce has developed a mythology in our league over the years. Urban myths circulate about not keeping score and no winners or losers of games. The league isn't quite that kumbaya, but they do put limits on how many runs a team can score in one inning and they do have a rule saying that if a pitcher walks four guys, he has to come out.

Again, these aren't bad ideas, but neither are they baseball. If your pitcher can't throw strikes and you choose to leave him in the game, then you have to live with the results.

Players and league officials more interested in making sure everyone has a positive experience are bound to water down the experience for everyone else.

But who am I to say? The guys in the Ponce league probably have a good time. They get a little exercise. They run around a little. They throw the ol' apple around the yard. And then they go home and forget about it. They don't lie awake in the terrible hours, turning the games over in their minds, lamenting the called third strike or the errant throw. They're sleeping.

The worst part about hitting that bouncer to the pitcher for the last out of season wasn't losing the championship. It wasn't the utterly unsatisfying tap I barely felt in my hands when the baseball made contact with the end of the bat. It wasn't even watching the Giants dogpile on each other right in the middle of the infield.

The worst part about hitting that bouncer back to the pitcher was knowing that George Bloch's changeup on the outside corner would haunt me all winter long. Running to first, three seconds after it happened, I saw it again in my head. I saw it when I plopped to the ground behind the bag. I saw it driving home from the ballpark. It was the same every time: Bloch's face as he let go of the ball, pretending to throw it as hard as he could. The ball traveling half as fast as I thought it would. My clueless swing. The tap.

Like a terrible song that rings in your head all day and night, the ghost of that pitch just kept showing up. And I just kept bouncing it back to the pitcher.

At home. Out for dinner. In meetings at my job. I could count on seeing that changeup five or six times a day. After about six weeks, I stopped talking about it, fearing my wife would think I might be obsessed. Or possessed. I was both. She caught me a few times, the last around Thanksgiving. I was muttering. "Damn. Dammit." I didn't know it was audible.

"What is it?" Deb asked.

"Huh? Oh. Nothing. It's nothing."

"It's that pitch, isn't it?"

"What? No. Jeez, no. That was months ago. Who cares?"

"You're muttering. It's still bothering you."

"C'mon. That's crazy."

But she was right. It was still bothering me. And no wonder.

I saw the pitch for the last time on Christmas morning. Five months after it happened, walking around my house in flannel pajamas, I stopped in my living room. I spread my feet shoulder length apart and held an imaginary bat in my stance. There it was. The ball came in, high and slow, spinning gently. I told myself to wait. Wait another instant. Wait for the ball to get closer. OK! Now! Swing! I swung my hips toward the fireplace and threw my hands at the pitch. I connected with the ghost, sending it arching gently over third base, bouncing down the line while A's baserunners spun madly around third, toward home plate.

If Bloch throws me that pitch again next year, I'll know what to do with it.

Index

Index

196